YALE

HISTORICAL PUBLICATIONS

MISCELLANY

IV

ISSUED UNDER THE DIRECTION OF THE
DEPARTMENT OF HISTORY
FROM THE INCOME OF
THE FREDERICK JOHN KINGSBURY
MEMORIAL FUND

THE READJUSTER MOVEMENT
IN VIRGINIA

BY

CHARLES CHILTON PEARSON, PH.D.

Professor of Political Science in Wake Forest College

GLOUCESTER, MASS.

PETER SMITH

1969

THE FREDERICK JOHN KINGSBURY
MEMORIAL PUBLICATION FUND

The present volume is the fifth work published by the Yale University Press on the Frederick John Kingsbury Memorial Publication Fund. This foundation was established August 3, 1912, by gifts to Yale University from Alice E. and Edith Davies Kingsbury, in memory of their father, Frederick John Kingsbury, LL.D., who was born in Waterbury, Connecticut, January 1, 1823, and died at Litchfield, Connecticut, September 30, 1910. Mr. Kingsbury was a graduate of Yale College in the Class of 1846, and an Alumni Fellow of the Yale Corporation from 1881 to 1899. The income of the Foundation is used "to promote the knowledge of American history and to associate the name of Frederick John Kingsbury with this study at Yale."

PREFACE

The half century just ended is the "Dark Age" of the South. Beginning with the attempt of Radicals to build upon the ruins of the old a foreign and ultra-democratic system, this period is probably now coming to its end in the educational and economic renaissance. And the over-lapping of the two ages may be studied today, throughout the older South, in farm and factory, state debt and schools, in poor white and aristocrat and "substantial citizen," and in the still uncertain status of the negro citizen and voter.

After the brief reign of Radicalism, during the "Dark Age," came a time of reaction, when "Confederate Brig-adiers" ruled, and the South was "solid." This was good. Times were exceedingly "hard," however, and heavy depression lay upon the spirit of the people. The excesses of Radicalism had disgusted many. So the gradual democratic advance discernible under the old system, to which war should have imparted a stimulus, was sharply checked.

During this time of reaction there occurred in most, if not all, of the Southern states a series of independent movements, some of which are still manifesting them-selves. The earlier of these movements were aided by the vote of the negro; the later, by the prejudice against him. In all, however, the leaders professed themselves inspired with zeal for the interests of the common white man. And it is not improbable that, studied closely and together, these movements may prove to have been, in origin and effects, democratic—an outworking of forces strengthened by war but restrained by reaction, and, however crude and sordid, harbingers of the renaissance.

One of the earliest and most far-reaching of these movements occurred in Virginia. It gathered about a state debt of long and interesting history. Eventually it produced a leader of national importance. This study, however, is not primarily an account either of the debt or of Mahone and his machine. It is, rather, a chapter in the history of Virginia, from the Civil War to the first administration of Grover Cleveland, in which some of the forces that moulded the present state are shown in their operation; and in the showing the "Readjuster" claim to liberalism, democracy, and progress is tested and due record made of the achievements and solid worth of those who stood for conservatism, aristocracy, and scrupulous honesty.

Hearty thanks are due to many who have aided me. Some have loaned materials or given information, specific acknowledgment of which is made below. The Virginia State Library staff have been untiringly helpful and courteous. Under the encouragement of Professor William A. Dunning the task had its beginning; if its completion proves worth while, the credit is due primarily to the sympathetic interest and practical assistance of Professor Max Farrand. In preparing the manuscript for the press Professor C. M. Andrews has placed me under lasting obligations.

C. C. Pearson.

Wake Forest, N. C.,
    January 1, 1917.

CONTENTS

CHAPTER I

THE STATE DEBT AND THE OLD RÉGIME,
1784-1867

From the Revolution to the Civil War one of the most important economic and social activities of the state of Virginia was the furtherance of a system of "Public Works."[1]
There were four main stages in the legislation under which this system was developed. It was inaugurated in 1784 when the state became, through purchase, a minority stockholder in corporations created for the improvement of the James and Potomac rivers. Among the sponsors for this beginning were a Newton, a Taylor, an Ambler, and a Southall, names still honored in Virginia; and a peculiar but characteristic mingling of business and sentiment appeared in the gift by the commonwealth of shares to "George Washington, esquire," in appreciation of his "unexampled merits" and his interest in enterprises which, the legislature thought, would be "the durable monuments of his glory."[2] To the policy thus begun a decided impetus was imparted in 1816 when all the state's holdings in

[1] There is no adequate study of the social and economic aspects of this system. Sydenstricker and Burger's *School History of Virginia* (1914) gives a brief but correct account based on the work of Mr. Sydenstricker which is still in manuscript. C. H. Ambler, in his *Sectionalism in Virginia from 1776 to 1861*, has described its political bearings in elaborate and scholarly fashion.

[2] W. W. Hening, *Statutes at Large*, XI, pp. 450, 510, 525. *Cf.* G. S. Callender, *Economic History of the United States*, p. 335 (quoting).

such companies were converted into one fund pledged for fifty years to the sole purpose of improving traffic and communication and managed by a special "Board of Public Works."[3] As the demands on this fund were greater than could be met by it, the legislature in 1838 directed the board to obtain money for all authorized improvements by selling state bonds.[4] This was an important step; for it meant that the state was entering, on credit, a business that was necessarily speculative. Here, practically, began the state debt. Twelve years later the fully developed policy was embodied in an act, still in force when the Civil War began, under which the board might borrow "from time to time, on the credit of the state of Virginia, such sums of money as may be needed to redeem the engagements of the state," which, of course, included not only new investments but also unearned interest.[5] In the development of this policy the western counties were most insistent.[6]

Behind this policy lay one great purpose, clearly indicated by the act of 1816 and adhered to with reasonable fidelity throughout the period. It was to knit together and develop the commonwealth as an economic unit. Such unity was demanded by the state's geographic divisions, the rivalry of outside markets, and the untouched wealth of the trans-Alleghany region.

[3] *Revised Code of the Laws of Virginia, 1819*, II, p. 201. The state's holdings in banks were placed in the same fund.

[4] *Code of Virginia, 1849*, p. 342; *Journal of the Senate of the Commonwealth of Virginia*, 1877-1878, Doc. XXIV, being a report of the committee on finance, prepared by Bradley T. Johnson. This journal will be cited hereafter as Sen. *Jour.*, the corresponding one of the House as House *Jour.* Documents are to be found (unless otherwise indicated) in the appendix of each.

[5] *Code of Virginia, 1860*, p. 386.

[6] Brief of Attorney-General William A. Anderson, in *Virginia vs. West Virginia, Supreme Court of the U. S., October term, 1909. Original Record*, p. 5.

Railroads, canals, turnpikes, were thought the best instrumentalities; so for these the state borrowed and spent. Powerful business interests, antagonistic sections, political parties all tried to shape the system in their own behalf, but none seriously opposed it as a whole. And when, in 1861, the policy was abruptly terminated, it had pre-empted the natural lines of commerce.[7]

The prevailing method of investment was determined in part by this dominant purpose and in part by the tendency of local capital to lock itself up in lands and labor. Instead of building and owning outright, the state endeavored to entice capital into transportation ventures by chartering stock companies therefor and itself becoming a partner in them. Terms too strict would have defeated the end; and so the state was generally less well secured than private undertakers; and often very poorly secured.[8] But the results obtained were distinctly creditable. For the thirty-five millions[9] which the state had invested down to 1861, it had secured, besides smaller improvements, a canal from Richmond to the Valley and a railroad system which cost nearly seventy millions and which was nearly half as long in miles as that of all New England.[10]

[7] Cf. Anderson, op. cit., and Ambler, Sectionalism, passim; Charles Bruce, Speech in the Senate of Virginia on the Internal Improvement Policy of the State, February 16, 1858 (1858).

[8] See terms of act of 1816, op. cit.; Messages and Documents, 1861-1862, No. 8; Bruce, op. cit.; Governor, Message, March 8, 1870. The governor's messages will be found in both Sen. Jour. and House Jour. under date of messages; they will be cited by date only.

[9] Round numbers will be used wherever exactness is not necessary to clearness.

[10] Expenditure figures are taken from Messages and Documents, 1861-1862, No. 8, table J; railroad figures from American Railroad Journal, January 5, 1861. $1,784,000 was spent by the state without the aid of a stock company. The total length of the railroad system was 2,483 miles;

The extent to which this policy dominated all other social and economic activities of the state finds striking illustration in its attitude toward education.[11]   A "Literary Fund," nominally created in 1810 by the segregation of certain small revenues, was firmly established in 1816 by turning into it the proceeds of a large war debt which the federal government had paid, the whole being solemnly pledged to educational purposes.   This fund appears to have been honestly handled and was gradually increased until in 1860 it amounted to over a million and three-quarters of dollars invested mainly in state bonds.   Most of the income from it and all the poll tax receipts after 1851 were regularly apportioned to the counties and towns.   But the education offered was intended only for confessed indigents selected in aristocratic fashion by a board of local officials.   The schools used were private with but nominal public supervision.   Only in rare cases was assistance extended beyond the most elementary stages.   Not unfittingly was the system often called the "pauper system,"[12] a name which expressed the fundamental idea of the ruling class that a man's children should be educated by himself, in proportion to his social status.   Any considerable education of the masses, they believed,

in operation, 1,805 miles.   The amount invested in railroads by the state was some twenty millions.   The estimates of B. T. Johnson (*op. cit.*) are somewhat larger.

[11] State Superintendent of Public Instruction, *Reports*, especially for 1871 and 1878, printed separately and in *Annual Reports of Officers, Boards and Institutions of the Commonwealth of Virginia*.   Reports in the latter collection will be cited (as above) under name of the reporting official or official board.   See also House *Jour.*, 1838, Doc. 4; *Documents and Messages*, 1861-1862, No. 7; A. D. Mayo, *Education in Southwest Virginia;* Ambler, *Sectionalism*, ch. IX; G. W. Dyer, *Democracy in the South before the Civil War*.   No account is taken here of appropriations to professional or collegiate institutions.

[12] This term was used in other states at similar stages of public school development.

must lead to unrest which could result only in disappointment or in "levelling." Only when charity absolutely demanded it should the state intervene.[13] Yet, despite the tremendous power of such opinion, the annual amount thus spent increased from $44,000 in 1836 to $214,000 in 1860, and the number thus "educated," from 18,000 to 62,000—which meant that by 1860 the state was paying the tuition of one-half of those at school within the limits of the present Virginia. Moreover, in some western counties and in parts of the older section open to outside influences, the desire for state aid had prompted experiments in schools supported jointly by state and local governments and free, or nearly free, to all. These facts, together with the reports sent in to Richmond by local officials, irregular and imperfect though they were, seem to demonstrate clearly that the old aristocratic idea was giving way before the new and democratic impulse.[14] Could a direct issue have been forced, the latter must have triumphed. But eastern Virginia had now become politically and financially committed to the policy of internal improvements, while the western part of the state, always the leader in democratic movements, was too much absorbed in its desire for more railroads and more turnpikes,[15] to put the matter to a test.

On the whole, fiscal conditions and prospects in 1860 appeared to be satisfactory. There was, indeed, a

[13] Professor Dyer thinks otherwise: ''The method of Virginia may be criticised, but the motive was thoroughly democratic,'' *Democracy in the South*, p. 77.

[14] Another defect, inherent in the dominant theory, was the lack of co-ordination and adequate supervision. Strongly backed attempts had been made to remedy this also.

[15] Ambler, *Sectionalism, passim*. Professor Ambler attributes the unusual activity in building public works from 1850 to 1860 to the program for a united South. *Ibid.*, 311.

bonded debt of $33,000,000.[16] But offsetting this were
assets of a face value of $43,000,000, consisting chiefly
of the stocks and bonds of the railroads and canals.[17]
As yet less than one-fifth of these were yielding the state
an income; but most of the rest, as most of the debt, had
been accumulated only within the last decade, and time
was needed to make extensions and develop the western
trade, for which purpose charters had already been
issued and appropriations authorized.[18] That the debt
had trebled within the last decade and would probably
continue to increase under the operation of the act of
1850 was certainly ominous. But, on the other hand, the
constitution adopted in 1850 removed old dangers by
forbidding the state to guarantee corporate liabilities
or release the corporations from their obligations to it.
The constitution also provided for a sinking fund which
must be adequate, safe, and unimpairable in times of
peace, and into which must be converted the proceeds
of any assets sold.[19] Back of debt and speculative
assets was a settled population of over a million and a
half, two-thirds of which was white, and property worth
over a billion dollars. From dividends and from taxes
on polls, incomes, property, and business licenses the
state derived an annual revenue of over four millions,[20]
of which less than one million was needed for the ordinary purposes of government.[21] Back of all this was a
record of fiscal honor which none was disposed to tarnish

[16] Exclusive of the bonds owned by the literary and sinking funds,
Messages and Documents, 1861-1862, No. 8. There was a small sterling
debt.

[17] *Ibid.*, table T.

[18] *Ibid.*, table K. There appears to have been no ''water'' in the stock
of these ''public works.''

[19] F. N. Thorpe, *American Charters, Constitutions, and Organic Laws*,
VII, 3841-3842. This will be cited as *Thorpe*.

[20] Auditor, *Report*, 1861-1862.

[21] *Cf.* p. 54.

by questioning the honesty of the debt or the state's ability to pay it. State bonds in the first half of 1860 sold above 90.[22]

When the Civil War was over, the state's great system of public works was an utter ruin.[23] The canal lay incomplete, dismantled, profitless—"a great gash across the heart of the commonwealth." Though, bit by bit, the railroads patched up their worn-out rails and rolling-stock, rebuilt burned bridges and depots, and opened for business, yet it was all too obvious that they must have time and a great deal of money before they either paid dividends or met the needs of the people.[24] Western Virginia, for the development of which these railroads had been built so largely, and to which the worn-out eastern counties had looked for a lightening of taxes, was now gone, a full third of the old state.

Sadly reduced, too, was the people's tax-paying capacity.[25] "By the abolition of slavery and of the 'Confederate debt,' " said the *Commercial and Financial Chronicle*,[26] "nearly the whole of the accumulated and available capital of the South was practically annihilated." Of the rest, that which had been invested directly in the public works brought little return or none, and that which had been invested in state bonds, perhaps

[22] For favorable opinion see *Journal of Banking, Currency and Finance*, January, 1860.

[23] Contemporary newspapers; "Personal Recollections."

[24] *American Railroad Journal*, July 1, 15, 29; September 9, 23; October 14; November 4, 1865; also, 1866, 1867, 1868, *passim*.

[25] An interesting report on the losses of war, made by a committee consisting of ex-Governor William Smith, W. T. Taliaferro, and T. J. Armstrong, and adopted by the House, January 13, 1877, was as follows: personal property, $116,000,000; realty, $121,000,000; internal improvements, $26,000,000; banking capital, $15,000,000; circulation, $12,000,000; state's interest in banks, $4,000,000; slaves and other property, $163,-000,000.

[26] January 18, 1868.

the greater part of the whole debt,[27] was shrunk two-thirds in market value. Farm lands, long deteriorating, now through the necessary change in labor system had become less desirable from a social point of view, and less productive, too, even where the ex-slave settled down on a wage or crop-sharing basis.[28] As offsets there were, indeed, high prices for tobacco, corn, and wheat, and a rise of land values in and about the towns, which was caused by the shifting of the native population and the incoming of outsiders.[29] But, despite the excellent credit of Virginia farmers abroad, to borrow on lands divorced from slaves was difficult.[30] Yet borrow one must for fences, for farming implements and livestock, for houses, for mills—for almost everything which four years of business stagnation and ruthless devastation could destroy. With state assets and the tax-paying power of the people fully two-thirds reduced, what hope was there for the payment of the public debt now increased by war time interest to $38,000,000?[31]

The legislature which faced this almost hopeless

[27] Governor, *Message*, December 4, 1865. In 1887 ex-Governor Peirpoint stated that 80 per cent was supposed to be owned in Virginia just after the war, E. H. Hancock, *Autobiography of John E. Massey*, p. 120 (cited hereafter as Massey, *Autobiography*). Wm. L. Royall, *History of the Virginia State Debt Controversy*, p. 6, and John P. McConnell, in *The South in the Building of the Nation*, I, p. 133, appear to hold a contrary opinion. The sale to outsiders was rapid. In 1874 it was estimated that only one-fourth was owned in Virginia, Second Auditor, *Report*, 1874.

[28] B. B. Munford, *Virginia's Attitude toward Slavery and Secession*, ch. 19; B. W. Arnold, *History of the Tobacco Industry in Virginia*, ch. 2.

[29] The increase in the number of whites at work was at least offset by the waste in the general transition; nor should the increase be estimated too highly, Callender, *Economic History*, p. 783, and Dyer, in *The South in the Building of the Nation*, X, ch. 9.

[30] See Ruffin in Richmond *Whig*, Sept. 25, 1874. *Cf.* below pp. 25-27, 44.

[31] Governor, *Message*, December 4, 1865. The literary and sinking funds are not included, and will not be in future statements of the amount of the debt.

situation in December, 1865, was the last one thoroughly characteristic of *ante-bellum* Virginia.[32] Its acts, therefore, are important not only as immediately affecting fiscal affairs but also as disclosing mental and moral attitudes, the stubborn yielding of which to changed conditions forms a large part of the history of the next generation.

Foremost among the important matters to which Governor Peirpoint called the attention of this legislature was the state debt, for the payment of the interest on which bondholders were "pressing." Several honorable courses lay open. The legislature might delay action pending a settlement with West Virginia, for which the organic laws of both states provided.[33] By so doing it would secure the aid of powerful private interests in compelling a settlement, and thus definitely limit the state's obligations. It might frankly recognize that the state was bankrupt and seek a compromise with creditors, for men afterwards said that fifty per cent in new bonds would have been

[32] Richmond *Enquirer*, March 3, 1866. Under Lincoln's plan of reconstruction as amended by Johnson the hitherto shadowy government of ''loyal'' Virginia, administered from Alexandria for the most part, was extended to all Virginia. Peirpoint was governor. The legislature was chosen on practically the same basis as before the war, Eckenrode, *Political Reconstruction of Virginia*, ch. 3. John B. Baldwin was speaker of the House.

[33] The constitution of West Virginia and the act of the ''loyal'' Virginia legislature assenting to the division of the state clearly created a contract between the two states under which their legislatures were to adjust the debt. The act of Congress admitting the new state ratified this contract. The secession convention at Wheeling, August 3, 1861, had specified terms of adjustment, but these were not mentioned in any of the above documents and were expressly repudiated by the constitution of ''loyal'' Virginia (*Thorpe*, VII, 3862). The United States Supreme Court decided in 1870 (11 *Wall.*, 39) that a contract had been created as above, and, in 1911, that the Wheeling terms were only a ''preliminary suggestion'' (220 *U. S.*, 1).

accepted.[34]   Instead, by act of March 2, 1866, the legislature not only assumed full responsibility for the entire *ante-bellum* principal but also authorized the funding of the entire war-time interest into bonds bearing the same rate of interest as the principal, payment of interest on the whole to begin the following year. This action was the utmost that any creditor asked. It was taken without a hint of improper influences and without recorded opposition.[35]

Chief among the reasons for this policy was a scrupulous regard for the state's unblemished fiscal record.[36] Another was the attitude toward West Virginia. Ignoring the tendency of fifty years[37] and the events of the last four years, the members of the legislature issued a confident "appeal to their brethren of West Virginia" for the "restoration of the ancient commonwealth of Virginia, with all her people, and up to her former boundaries," and appointed a commission to effect it. Only after the commission had failed in this effort was it to treat for a division of the public debt and assets.[38]

At the second session of the legislature the debt question was re-opened. West Virginia had taken no action. Crops had been poor. Private debts were pressing and there was talk of scaling them. Why, men asked here

[34] A very interesting suggestion was offered by J. Willcox Brown, later a banker of Virginia and Baltimore, that after assuming the debt and levying taxes therefor the state should invite some English bankers to act as trustees, take over her assets and make the best possible terms. Such a course might have changed the entire *post-bellum* history, *Brown Papers*.

[35] *Acts of the General Assembly of the State of Virginia, passed in 1865-1866*, p. 79; House and Senate *Journals*, 1865-1866, index; Governor, *Message*, December 4, 1865; contemporary *Whig, Enquirer*.

[36] This record was mentioned by foreign creditors time and again. The faith of English business concerns in Virginia farmers was similarly strong. See "Financial Relief That Might Have Been," *Brown Papers*.

[37] Ambler, *Sectionalism, passim*.

[38] *Acts*, 1865-1866, p. 453 (being joint resolution of February 28, 1866).

and there, should not the public debt be scaled in proportion to losses? In this "wild talk" lay the germ of repudiation.[39] But the legislature formally reprobated such sentiments, discussed nothing more dangerous than declining responsibility for West Virginia's share—a suggestion endorsed by some creditors—and, finally, regretting its inability to do more, authorized the payment of four instead of six per cent interest for the current year, "that being the amount which this state feels obliged to pay until there is a settlement of accounts between this state and West Virginia."[40] Holders of coupon bonds could, of course, receive full interest by presenting their coupons for taxes or other state dues, and the same privilege was accorded holders of registered bonds.[41] To meet the interest voted and the expenses of government, the relatively high tax of thirty cents was imposed on personalty and on realty as valued in 1856.[42] No pressure appears to have been

[39] Governor, *Message*, December 3, 1866; Auditor, *Report*, 1866; *American Annual Cyclopedia*, 1866, article "Virginia." The last (which became Appleton's with 1876) will be cited as *Annual Cyc.*, and all references not otherwise indicated will be to "Virginia." The *Whig*, however, declared that it had heard of no desire to scale the public debt prior to the governor's message.

[40] *Acts*, 1866-1867, December 20, March 21; editorial résumé of daily debates in *Whig* and *Enquirer*. For positions of these papers on the debt see *Enquirer*, December 5, 1866, and *Whig*, March 19, 20, 22, 1867. The vote on the act appropriating four per cent was: House, 58 to 18; Senate, 17 to 2. James Branch, of Thomas Branch & Co., bankers and brokers of Richmond, suggested a compromise with creditors on the basis of 6 per cent bonds for seventy per cent of the debt and certificates of West Virginia's indebtedness for the rest, *Enquirer*, February 4, 1867. The best people of West Virginia, in the opinion of Mr. Septimus Hall who has given this phase much study, desired at this time to make a settlement.

[41] Act of April 25, 1867.

[42] Thirty cents on each $100, the customary statement of the tax rate in this state. Valuation for taxation was called "assessing"; this was made annually for personalty, every five years for realty. There were other taxes.

used to obtain these results. Yet by this time it was
certain that the state would be degraded, as no state had
ever been degraded under the Congressional reconstruction measures. Moreover, bonds were rapidly passing
out of the hands of native owners. Hints were, indeed,
thrown out to the North by the *Whig*[43] that repudiation
of private and public debts might be invited. But the
legislature appeared blind alike to economic conditions
and to the possibilities of compromise, sensitive only to
the old ideas of honor.

Viewed from the debt standpoint only, the question of
the state's assets[44] was quite simple: Should they be sold
at once to reduce the immediate burden or should they
be retained as a source of future revenue? Past policy
and the prevailing confidence in the future suggested the
latter; the burden of the interest and the cheapness of
state bonds urged the former. But as these assets consisted chiefly of the stocks and bonds of railroads
within the state, the transportation problem must also
be considered.

Under the old policy the natural routes for great
railroads had been pre-empted.[45] From north to south
connecting short lines crossed the state at two points.
One could go from Norfolk on the coast to Bristol in
the far west by using three roads—the Norfolk and
Petersburg, the Southside, and the Virginia and Tennessee. From Richmond to Covington in Alleghany
County ran the Virginia Central. Charters had been
issued and appropriations authorized to continue these
westward lines, the one through Cumberland Gap, the
other through the undeveloped Greenbrier county to the

---

[43] December 5, 12, 1866; March 20, 1867.

[44] For condition, see Governor, *Message*, December 4, 1865.

[45] With the exception of that of the Virginian Railroad, recently con-
structed.

Ohio, both seeking the Mississippi. Among these and the other numerous short lines a fair degree of unity had been attained, because through the Board of Public Works, as a kind of holding company, the state subscriptions had been made and the state stock voted.[46] But all of these roads now needed money,[47] and this the state could no longer supply directly, or indirectly.[48] The needs of commerce, therefore, seemed to demand, as the governor kept insisting, that the old policy should give way to private ownership and consolidated management.[49]

To this problem of the state's assets the legislature addressed itself at greater length and with more heat than to any other. Advocates of immediate reduction of the debt principal, supported by private interests, urged a general sale to the highest bidder.[50] But it was too much, so frankly to declare Virginia bankrupt and so completely to reverse the policy of the past. Most of the roads were, indeed, permitted to buy out the state's interests in them. They were permitted also to combine their managements. But each permission was carefully hedged about with restrictions and guarantees

[46] F. A. Magruder, *Recent Administration in Virginia*, p. 147.

[47] *Cf. American Railroad Journal*, October 23; November 4; December 16, 1865.

[48] *Thorpe*, VII, 3861-3862.

[49] There is nowhere a full description of the situation, see Governor, *Message*, December, 1865 and 1866; *Enquirer*, January 30, 31; March 7; Richmond *Dispatch*, January 23, 31, February 6, 23; *Whig*, March 6, April 19, 1867.

[50] A bill to this effect attached as a rider to the act of March 21, 1867, for payment of interest on the public debt passed the House, *Jour.*, 1866-1867, extra sess., pp. 63-64. For the long fight against outside control, see Ambler, *Sectionalism*, index, under "Baltimore and Ohio." Objections are succinctly given in *Whig*, December 8, 1866; see also *Enquirer*, March 21, 22; *Dispatch*, March 21, 1867. Motives appear in various resolutions, *e.g.*, House *Jour.*, 1865-1866, pp. 65, 377; *ibid.*, 1866-1867, pp. 12, 132, 208.

intended to prevent monopoly and to secure long-desired extensions, quite in conformity with the state's former policy.[51]

Similarly, other acts of this legislature showed it to be following old prevailing tendencies, often failing to grasp or deliberately ignoring new conditions. No attempt was made to compel an equitable compromise of old private debts, the security for which was gone in whole or in part. Instead, acts merely staying their collection until 1869 were passed.[52] With loanable funds commanding from ten to fifty per cent, pleas for a relaxation of the six per cent legal rate were refused.[53] As slavery had been patriarchal, so now equally patriarchal was the legislation directly affecting the freedman: if the latter stayed at home and attended to his work, he was better protected than the ignorant white; if he insisted upon being idle, he was practically remanded to servitude; if he committed crime, his own race could testify for or against him, but only before white judges and juries.[54] Though old appropriations to collegiate and professional schools were revived, elementary education was neglected.[55]

Outside the legislature, also, old forces reasserted themselves. The ex-planter paid his negroes a share of

[51] Out of such acts, when supplemented by further concessions, were to grow the Atlantic, Mississippi and Ohio, the Virginia Midland, and the Chesapeake and Ohio, Acts of April 18, February 14, March 1, 1867.

[52] Acts of March 2, 1866; March 2, 1867.

[53] Governor, *Message*, December, 1866; *Whig*, January 29; February 3, 1866. J. Willcox Brown gives details of an English scheme to lend five million dollars at six and one-half per cent on security of Virginia farm lands which was blocked by this refusal, *Brown Papers*.

[54] *Acts*, 1865-1867, pp. 83, 84, 89, 91; Eckenrode, *Political Reconstruction*, ch. 3; McConnell, *Negroes and their Treatment*, chs. 6, 7, 8.

[55] An argument advanced against the levying of taxes for debt interest at this time was that the proceeds might be used by the federal government to support public schools, *Whig*, March 20, 1867.

the crop instead of board and clothes. Grown men studied law as they would have been doing three or four years before had there been no war. Among the newspapers, the *Enquirer* and the *Whig* again dictated public opinion, seldom agreeing. Far behind, the *Dispatch* gathered news and talked business. Men wanted to revive their old party lines.[56] When a party convention met, there was the old oligarchical dominance.[57] Nowhere do we meet with new ideas, nowhere with an adequate appreciation of what had happened; but everywhere we find infinite patience with the ex-slave, a stubborn clinging to what was deemed honor, and a strange capacity for silent, cheerful suffering.

Thus before the Civil War Virginia concentrated her economic activities upon a system of public works, with the result that in 1861 she possessed assets in railroads and canals of great potential value but offset by a very large public debt. There was an increasing demand for state participation in public education and the like. But this demand was met only partially because it conflicted at once with the policy of internal improvements and with the individualistic and aristocratic ideas of the ruling class. Consequently, state expenditures were small and taxes light, and the credit of the state was excellent. The first legislature after the war was representative of the old régime. Though the balance between debt and assets had been fearfully upset, this legislature recognized the debt as absolutely binding and tried to provide for interest payment. Most of the railroad assets, it permitted to pass into private hands but under careful restrictions. It made no provision whatever for schools or charities. In these and most other

[56] Below, p. 20.
[57] Below, p. 20.

respects the old ruling class showed itself to be adhering to past policies and standards. New ideas appearing were the consolidation of railroads, which was grudgingly and partially accepted, and the scaling of public and private debts, which was not seriously considered.

CHAPTER II

RADICALISM, 1867-1869

Hard upon this conservative legislature came the "Radical" constitutional convention of 1867-1869.[1] Called to "reconstruct" the state according to Congressional mandate, this convention in both its membership and its acts savored much of outside influences, and was characterized by ignorance and self-seeking. None the less, both its acts and its membership indicated, in however absurdly exaggerated form, social forces released or newly created that would have to be dealt with in the future.

Negroes, "scalawags," and "carpet-baggers" predominated, with only a few scions of the old régime to hector and oppose them. Unmindful of economic conditions, they struck "frugality" from the ancient Bill of Rights; but mindful of the freedmen to whom they owed their unwonted prominence, they inserted the "equal civil and political rights and public privileges" of all citizens.[2] These two alterations give the key to their plan of government.

[1] "Radical" and "Republican" were ordinarily used without distinction, and will be so used herein. This sketch, based on Eckenrode, *Political Reconstruction*, the convention journals, and the contemporary Richmond newspapers, is intended to show only the popular and expansive features of the constitution.

[2] Section 15 of the Bill of Rights as adopted in 1851 read: "That no free government, or the blessings of liberty, can be preserved to any people but by a firm adherence to justice, moderation, temperance, frugality, and virtue, and by a frequent recurrence to fundamental principles." Compare this with section 17 in the document as adopted in 1869. Section 20

Suffrage was to be based on manhood; jury service and office-holding, on suffrage.[3]   Where before some twenty officials had served the average county's needs, there was now to be a minimum of forty-eight, all elected for short terms and mostly by "townships" or smaller territorial divisions so that power might not gravitate into strong hands and "the people" lose their rights. For similar reasons judicial power was transferred from the old county board of justices to a county judge, and above him was the circuit court, above it the supreme court, forming a complex and costly system.   All of these judges were dependent upon the legislature for appointment, salary, and possibly tenure.   The legislature was also empowered to appoint all administrative officials except three, including all school officials, the Board of Public Works, and such other boards as it might be pleased to establish.   Instead of the old system of public aid doled out to indigents for education, a uniform system of schools, free to all classes, adequately supervised, and liberally supported by specified funds and taxes, was to be established at once, and by 1876 extended equally and fully to all the counties and towns. The burden of taxation should no longer fall upon the poor; for the state might levy no poll tax above one dollar, and the local government none above fifty cents, and all other taxation should be *ad valorem*.[4]

Significant for the future was the attitude of the convention toward debts.   The wild talk of 1866[5] now took the form of many resolutions offered by Radical mem-

of the latter reads: "That all citizens of the state are hereby declared to possess equal civil and political rights and public privileges."

[3] For the attempted disqualification of Confederates see below.

[4] A few specified license taxes and cases where values could not be ascertained form exceptions to the general principle.   Business capital and incomes over $600 were taxed as other property.

[5] Above, p. 10.

bers to scale or repudiate private obligations, which
resulted in an unusual number of petty exemptions. In
close connection with these resolutions were similar,
though less vigorous, attacks upon the public debt.[6]
Efforts of conservative men, including some Radicals,
secured recognition of the latter in the constitution.[7]
But between the policy of protecting a huge public debt
and the policy of expensive and popular government
there was, under the impoverished conditions prevailing,
an incompatibility as striking as that between the old
and the new elements of the convention.

Had the Radicals been allowed to carry out the terms
of this constitution, rampant democracy would unquestionably have had full play for years to come, and one
can only conjecture the extremes to which it would
probably have gone. But by inserting clauses disfranchising many ex-Confederates,[8] the convention, alarmed
and disgusted almost the entire white population, and,
as the whites were in a decided majority, made possible
the victory of moderate men. Two steps were taken in
reaching this end.

The first to move were the extreme men of the old
school. Confronted with the probable loss not only of
their political power and their private property but also
of their highly prized civilization, and fearful of "Africanization" and "Yankeeizing,"[9] they determined to
defeat the constitution at the polls even though they

6 The printed journals are incomplete and unindexed. See, however,
pp. 150, 442-444, 519, 705.

7 Thorpe, VII, 3894-3895. This was contrary to the general rule in the
new constitutions of the Southern states, Dunning, *Reconstruction*, p. 207.

8 Thorpe, VII, 3876. The "test oath" (*ibid.*, 3877) would have excluded
all ex-Confederates from office.

9 This feeling is vividly expressed in private correspondence of the time,
see *Ruffner Papers; Memoirs of Gov. William Smith;* T. J. Johnson, *Robert
E. Dabney.*

knew that this would probably mean a long continuation of military rule. Meeting in state conventions dominated by two or three *ante-bellum* leaders, they planned a complete organization under the name "Conservative," and nominated a state ticket.[10] Their success would ultimately have meant no extravagance, no corruption, and no repudiation; no democratic local government and no concentration of power in the legislature; no common schools, no extensive public charities; no jury service or office-holding for the negroes. An aristocratic and individualistic society, with as little governmental activity as possible and that little directed by the fittest, was the remedy for the distempers of the times thus boldly prescribed a second time by "Bourbons."[11]

To avoid the dilemma of negro rule on one side or military rule on the other, a "new movement" was begun. Before the elections for the constitutional convention, many substantial citizens, aided by the ardent pro-Southern *Whig,* had already given strong evidence of their desire to "co-operate" with the Republican party for the restoration of the state to the Union on the basis of universal suffrage and equal civil and political rights. The movement, however, lacked distinctive leadership and died almost still-born.[12] After the convention and the Republican victory in the election of 1868, the idea revived in the form of an agree-

[10] *Dispatch* and *Whig,* December 12, 13, 1867; May 7, 8, 1868. Col. R. E. Withers was nominated for governor. Raleigh T. Daniel, John B. Baldwin, and A. H. H. Stuart were leaders. Their dominance was, of course, due to the crisis and the trust imposed in them. It was exercised largely through a "committee on business," named by the chairman, which shaped all matters before the convention, including party organization. *Cf.* below, pp. 39, 49.

[11] Though the term "Bourbon" was little used until later, it will be employed here to designate the ultra-conservatives and their ideas. We should remember that many changed their views soon after this.

[12] Eckenrode, *Political Reconstruction,* ch. 5.

ment between groups of moderate leaders in both parties, heartily supported by the *Whig,* for the adoption of the constitution without the disfranchising clause, and the election of respectable Republican state officials and a moderate legislature.[13]   Having obtained permission, through the favor of President Grant, to vote for the constitution without the objectionable clause, these men next induced the "True Republican" faction[14] to endorse their plan and nominate for governor Gilbert C. Walker, a carpet-bagger Republican, but a moderate and intelligent man, strongly connected in Congressional circles.   Though many Bourbons objected bitterly to this procedure, all of them yielded to its manifest advantages (some perhaps with mental reservations),[15] and withdrew their candidate.[16]   Thereupon the masses of the whites rallied under the old name, "Conservative," in support of the movement.   In this way originated the Conservative party of the future.

The significance of these events lay, undoubtedly, in the preference of the white masses for moderation instead of for Radicalism or Bourbonism.   Pregnant

[13] For full narrative accounts see *A Narrative of the Leading Incidents,* etc., by A. H. H. Stuart, who is credited by Eckenrode (*Political Reconstruction,* ch. 7) with having initiated the move; "New Virginia," in *Whig,* February 4, 1885; and Frank G. Ruffin in *Dispatch,* October 30, 1880, emphasizing Mahone's share.   For national interest and approval see New York *Herald,* January 3, 16; April 8, 29; New York *Times,* April 9, 1869.

[14] *Cf.* Rhodes, *History of the United States since 1850,* VI, 304.   Mr. Rhodes's quotation cannot be applied to this faction in Virginia.

[15] *Enquirer, passim;* R. E. Withers, *Autobiography of an Octogenarian,* pp. 275 ff.; *Memoirs of Gov. William Smith,* pp. 263, 269, 276.   The following ironic telegram (New York *Times,* July 8, 1869) to President Grant from R. T. Daniel excited mirth among Richmond Bourbons: "I congratulate you upon the triumph of your policy in Virginia.   The gratitude of the people for your liberality is greatly enlivened by the overwhelming majority by which that policy prevails."

[16] At a meeting of the old Conservative central committee and county "superintendents," *Annual Cyc.,* 1869.

with meaning for the future, also, and of no little immediate importance, was the fact that the most efficient
of the new leaders were city men and represented large
business interests. Thus, Walker, at this time a banker
of Norfolk, was interested in Virginia bonds. Franklin
Stearns, a Republican who had been considered for the
gubernatorial nomination, appears to have been closely
associated with large railroad interests centering in
Richmond, with which the management of the *Dispatch*,
likewise a supporter of the movement, was also soon
associated. Though attracting little public notice, none
was more active than Gen. William Mahone, president
of the Atlantic, Mississippi and Ohio Railroad. To him
and to his numerous correspondents the success of
Walker meant the success of ''consolidation,'' for the
nominees of both the Radicals and the Bourbons were
bitterly hostile to his plans.[17]

Despite the concessions of the whites, the negroes
voted by a very large majority for the Radical candidate
and disfranchisement. None the less, the ''new movement'' won an easy victory. Under the deft guidance
of Walker and his advisers[18] and with pledges to abide

---

[17] Below, p. 27. Col. R. E. Withers, the Bourbon nominee, was closely
associated with the extreme Lynchburg opposition to Mahone's control of
the Va. & Tenn., Withers, *Autobiography*, pp. 242 ff. Governor Wells, the
Radical nominee, had tried to sell this road to the B. & O. Railroad (Eckenrode, *Political Reconstruction*, p. 117) and he appears to have received
B. & O. support during this campaign. Among those who assisted Mahone
were: J. F. Slaughter, of Lynchburg; Geo. W. Bolling, of Petersburg; V. D.
Groner and R. H. Glass, of Norfolk, Robert M. Hughes, of Abingdon. See
also letters of John W. Johnston, G. K. Gilmer, of Richmond; H. W.
Holliday, and ex-Governor Peirpoint, *Mahone Papers*. Walker's influence
over Grant appears to have been exercised through ''Chandler.'' James
Barbour, brother of the president of the Orange & Alexandria Railroad,
and Robert Ould, who represented Richmond's interests in the Canal, both
competitors of the A. M. & O., opposed the move.

[18] *Whig*, October 10, 12; *Dispatch*, October 2, 8, 1869; Eckenrode,
Political Reconstruction, p. 126.

by the essentially democratic features of the expurgated constitution,[19] Virginia returned finally and fully to the Union in January, 1870.

We have seen, then, that the reconstruction constitution was framed by adventurers in the interests of the "mud sills of society." It sought to create complete equality by such devices as manhood suffrage and jury service, numerous elective local offices, taxation according to wealth, and state support of common schools and charities. The sponsor for these ideas was the Radical, or Republican, party, but they were also accepted as a matter of expediency by a new party, called "Conservative," and supported by the bulk of the whites. "Bourbons," that is, advocates of the old-time policies, opposed this course. While insisting upon these democratic ideas, some Radicals of the constitutional convention endeavored to scale both public and private debts, but without success. Ratification of the new constitution was accomplished through the combination of the Conservatives with a wing of the Republican party. This combination was effected by city capitalistic leaders, and to it (and them) was entrusted the inauguration of the new régime.

[19] *Code of 1870*, preface. These included suffrage and public education. *Cf.* Dunning, *Essays on Civil War and Reconstruction*, pp. 347 ff.

CHAPTER III

"RESTORATION OF CREDIT," 1870-1871

When the first legislature of reconstructed Virginia met in January, 1870, twenty-seven negroes had seats. The absence of well-known faces was marked—acts of Congress and the exigencies of the campaign had kept them at home. Men said—some with obvious effort—that it was perhaps well; for the young men and new men could more easily forget the past and face the pressing problems which war and reconstruction had created or complicated.[1]

Chief among these problems was the serious economic and fiscal situation. The state debt now amounted to over $45,000,000[2]—$36 for each person, $62 for each white. Transition from the old to the new transportation policy awaited completion; meantime the state's assets paid little dividend and commerce was hampered. There were, however, some signs of improvement. Small farms for the landless were beginning to be created from the great estates; men unaccustomed to work were putting their hands literally to the plow; in some parts

[1] *Dispatch, Whig, Enquirer*, October 5-12, 1869. *Cf.* Mayes, *L. Q. C. Lamar*, p. 131. This legislature had in the fall of 1869 completed the reconstruction process. Its composition was: Senate, 30 Conservatives and 13 Radicals (6 negroes); House, 95 Conservatives (3 negroes) and 42 Radicals (18 negroes), *Annual Cyc.*, 1869.

[2] Under the act of March 2, 1866, "a large proportion" of interest accrued by January 1, 1867, had been funded. Under act of March 21, 1867 (above, pp. 10, 11) four per cent interest had been paid in 1867 and two per cent in 1869. Between these dates the taxes were not fully collected and government expenses were high, Governor, *Message*, March 8, 1870.

old industries were taking on new life—truck-farming, for example, in the Norfolk region, the tonging and planting of oysters in the Chesapeake's tributaries, and cattle-raising in the southwest.[3] Favored by this activity and by immigration from the north and from other parts of the state, seventeen counties and all the cities but two showed greater realty values than in 1860.[4] The masses of the people appeared cheerful, glad, for all the changes, to be back at peaceful work again.[5] But the "good times" immediately succeeding the war had already begun to pass away.[6] Protected against old debts by stay laws, men had created a fictitious prosperity by making new loans, often at usurious rates. Now stay laws were unconstitutional, but the debts remained. The Richmond *Enquirer* gravely argued that "reason and true statesmanship dictate a compulsory scale of 'ante bellum' private debt from its apparent to its true value," and public meetings endorsed the suggestion.[7] Prices of farm products were declining

[3] "Personal Recollections."

[4] The basis of these estimates is the assessed values of 1860 (being the figures of 1856 corrected in 1860) and of 1870. Petersburg and Fredericksburg showed losses. Auditor, *Report*, 1871.

[5] *Ibid.;* tone of the press; "Personal Recollections"; *Ruffner Papers;* Johnson, *Dabney.*

[6] Tobacco production was 123,968,000 pounds in 1860, 114,480,000 in 1866, 43,761,000 in 1870. This decrease was coincident with a heavy federal tax, Arnold, *Tobacco Industry*, ch. 2. The price of bright tobacco, very high in 1865-1867, decreased thereafter, while the corn and pork imported by the planters were high, *Whig*, March 8, December 8, 1870. In non-tobacco growing sections the high price of corn was offset by the low price of wheat, *ibid.*, March 8, 17. There had been a succession of disastrous floods in the James and Shenandoah valleys; also droughts. *Annual Cyc.*, 1865-1870; Governor, *Message*, December 7, 1870. For negro exodus see *Enquirer*, February 17; March 19 to 25; *Whig*, April 20, 1870; for transition to town, P. A. Bruce, *Rise of the New South*, ch. 30; for the optimistic view of an intelligent English tourist, Robert Somers, *The Southern States Since the War.* Cf. State Grange, *Proceedings*, 1874.

[7] *Thorpe*, VII, 3896; *Enquirer*, February 17, March 19, 1870.

and production was increasing but slowly, sometimes actually decreasing. Negro laborers were leaving or talking of leaving, and even though they remained, land in most regions had not yet become profitable. In each of seventy-four counties, not including cities, realty values were distinctly smaller than in 1860, their shrinkage totalling probably over $10,000,000.[8]

To meet this situation, Governor Walker urged[9] a "restoration of credit" policy. Let the entire $45,000,-000 of debt, he said, be funded into uniform coupon bonds bearing the same rate of interest as the old, the coupons being declared on their face receivable for taxes and other public dues. Complete the exchange of the state's interest in public works for state bonds. Curtail expenses. Tax all property at its *true* value,[10] and reach out for other sources of revenue possible under the new constitution. The honor of the state would thus be preserved and its credit restored. Then grant liberal franchises under general laws, unhamper the private interest rate and, while making concessions in the case of old debts, secure the creditor by "prompt and effective remedies for the enforcement of his rights." Private credit, as the basis of individual prosperity, would follow.

The spirit in which these recommendations were made—its extravagant optimism[11] and its sympathetic appreciation of state pride—received from the press the

8 Assessed realty values for the entire state showed a loss of some fifteen millions, or about five per cent (currency); but the cities and favored counties showed an increase of nineteen millions.

9 *Message*, March 8, 1870; December 6, 1871.

10 This he assumed to be the same as the "true value" given by the census of 1860.

11 For example: "We have a canal which, when completed, will prove as valuable an adjunct to commerce as the far-famed Suez Canal. . . . A Southern Pacific railroad has been projected with its eastern terminus at Norfolk, and I doubt not it will be built."

heartiest commendation and helped to conciliate or silence elements hitherto in opposition.[12] The legislature responded readily. It provided for the funding of the debt, adopted a liberal railroad policy, and enacted a tax law of greater reach than any heretofore passed. It took the first step toward repealing the constitutional restriction of the contractual private interest rate to twelve per cent.[13] It gave liberal interpretation to the exemption provisions of the constitution, especially as regards private debts contracted prior to the end of the war.[14] It left no room for a Radical reaction or interference of the federal government, for it set in motion the local government machinery, enacted laws for the protection of suffrage, and created an elaborate and up-to-date public school system.[15] Because of their future bearings, the first two of these acts require more extended notice.

Among the railroad acts of the legislature of 1865-1867 was one permitting Gen. William Mahone and others to merge, under careful restrictions, the managements of the three lines from Norfolk to Bristol and to build extensions with a view to connecting eventually the seaboard with the Mississippi and the Ohio. This was the Atlantic, Mississippi and Ohio Railroad. This plan, however, had met with opposition, both from those who opposed consolidation on theoretical grounds and from those with conflicting business interests. As had been expected from the alignment of forces in 1869, Mahone at first received the co-operation of Governor Walker in forcing through the legislature, with the aid of the Republican vote, an act granting the A. M. & O.

[12] *Whig, Dispatch, Enquirer,* and citations in each, March 9-11, December 8, 9, 1870; above, p. 21.

[13] *Acts,* 1869-1870, p. 19.

[14] Act of June 27, 1870.

[15] Act of July 11, 1870; below, p. 60.

valuable privileges and completely crushing the opposition within the consolidating roads.[16] Others, apparently with Mahone's assistance, received similar charters.[17] But these acts were soon seen to be only a part of the governor's "free railroad" policy. "Wherever," he said in his next annual message,[18] "a railroad, or a canal, or a transportation company, is needed, and people can be found who will invest the necessary capital, let the enterprise be organized and completed." Since this policy involved the sale of such of the state's assets as had not already been disposed of, a bill to that effect was introduced. But Mahone, deeming the policy dangerous to A. M. & O. interests, fought it. The *Enquirer,* which had recently been purchased by the Pennsylvania Central Railroad and reorganized under Richmond business men and politicians for the acknowledged purpose of advocating "Free Railroads" and the "maintenance of public and private credit of the state,"[19] urged the bill's

[16] Act of June 17, 1870; *Enquirer,* March 3, 16, 18, 20, 1871. The state's interest might be bought by the consolidated road for $4,000,000 in state bonds at par, payable in installments beginning January 1, 1885. The security for the purchase should be a mortgage on the consolidated road second to a first mortgage of $15,000,000. The proceeds of the latter were to be used for building an extension through Cumberland Gap and for certain minor purposes. To the opposition above noted (p. 22) had now been added certain Richmond men, who were interested in an air-line from Richmond to Lynchburg, and the East Tennessee, Virginia and Georgia Railroad represented by John B. Baldwin.

[17] Acts of July 11, 1870 (Richmond and Danville); March 24 (Chesapeake and Ohio); January 14, March 28, 31 (Orange and Alexandria), 1871. Mahone appears to have reached an agreement with the Baltimore and Ohio interests, which were closely connected with the Orange and Alexandria, Letter of W. W. Wood, November 16, 1871, *Mahone Papers.*

[18] December 7, 1870.

[19] *Enquirer,* March 21; *Whig,* November 10, 1871. The *Enquirer* made no denial of the *Whig's* charge, "Are not six-sevenths of the *Enquirer* stock held in Pennsylvania?" Probably Governor Walker's political interests were to be looked after by the *Enquirer* in return for his support; certainly he had some close connection with the *Enquirer's* management in

passage. So did the *Dispatch*, the owner of which was an interested party.[20] Opposing it was the *Whig*, whose traditional attitude was to fight outside control and the diversion of trade from Virginia centers, and which, through A. M. & O. patronage, was gradually passing under Mahone's control.[21] Each side maintained an extensive lobby—an agency scarcely known before in Virginia, and each had legislators avowedly in its pay.[22] In the melée Mahone lost the negro vote and the bill was passed.[23]

Meanwhile there had come from the joint committee on finance a bill for funding the state debt, afterwards commonly known as "the Funding Act." It was the governor's bill in every point[24] save that interest-bearing

1874, Walker to Ruffner, September 4, *Ruffner Papers*, December 31, 1883. The *State* reprinted from the Chicago *Tribune* a letter of C. P. Huntington in which he spoke of Walker as "a slippery fellow, and I rather think in Scott's interest." See also letters of R. F. Walker (1872), in *Mahone Papers*.

[20] Act of March 28, 1871. The short lines from Washington south through Richmond were the main bone of contention. Some were primarily interested in the Carolina trade (*Dispatch*, March 10, 1871); others, in a trunk line north and south.

[21] Mahone appears to have negotiated for the purchase of the *Whig* in 1868 without success; yet from that year records of its business were regularly sent him. The *Whig's* editor asserted (March 4, 1872) that his views were reached independently and in ignorance of Mahone's. A total of $77,200 was paid the *Whig* by the A. M. & O., *Dispatch*, October 11, 1879.

[22] John Goode, Jr., represented Mahone (*Dispatch*, February 10, 1870; *New Virginia*, in *Whig*, January 3, 1885), but the charge that he was in the pay of Mahone is based on insufficient evidence; Walter Taylor and A. B. Cochran, the Pennsylvania interests (*Enquirer*, November 4, 1871); Gen. Bradley T. Johnson (who was not at this time in the legislature), John Lyons, and John W. Jenkins, a Radical lawyer of Richmond, the Richmond interests (*Dispatch*, February 15, 1872). The A. M. & O. paid $13,900 apparently for lobbying in addition to sums paid the *Whig*, *op. cit.*, 1879.

[23] Act of March 28, 1871. For convenient later account of the whole affair see *Dispatch*, June 16, 27; August 7, 8, 1877. The contemporary papers are full of it.

[24] Above; also speech of Walker, in *Dispatch*, October 3, 1877.

coupons instead of bonds were to be issued for one-third of the debt, for which "payment . . . will be provided in accordance with such settlements as shall hereafter be made between the states of Virginia and West Virginia."[25] Obsessed by a sense of obligation to the governor, overwhelmed by other duties, and involved in the railroad war, legislators could give to this bill no adequate study. Nor did they receive light from public discussion. The *Dispatch* and General Mahone kept discreetly silent. The *Enquirer,* indeed, favored the bill, and the *Whig* opposed it; but their arguments were clouded with references to each other's railroad and political intentions, and weakened by their complete reversal of opinion within four months.[26] At the very close of the session, having previously passed the Senate, this measure was railroaded through the House, receiving the votes of just half of the Conservatives and all of the Republicans but one.[27]

Thus the "restoration of credit" policy, balanced against and protected by a careful observance of the democratic ideas of the constitution, was enacted into law. Under its operation important business connections were formed with the North in which men of all shades of political opinion participated, and before these illiberalism of all kinds was certain to give way. Almost the entire state press[28] and the outside world endorsed the policy as economically correct. Yet several consid-

[25] In the opinion of Mr. Septimus Hall (previously quoted) Walker and the railroad interests blocked a settlement with West Virginia lest the latter demand a share of Virginia's assets and so delay railroad consolidation; and the opinion became fixed in West Virginia that no settlement would ever be demanded.

[26] Compare editorials in December, 1870, with those of March, 1871.

[27] Act of March 30, 1871; contemporary *Whig, Dispatch, Enquirer;* Ruffin, *Facts,* etc.; *Journals* of both houses, March, 1871. John W. Daniel and James Stubbs protested vigorously against the procedure.

[28] *Whig,* January 9, 1873.

erations might well have given pause to the men behind this policy.

(1) The state's most valuable fiscal assets had been contracted away upon terms that were inadequate if the grantee prospered, insecure if he did not prosper. No special privileges of the old railroads, such as exemption from taxation, proper enough under the former system, had been surrendered. No provision for control over transportation to take the place of the old method had been made. Such defects invited, if they did not compel, railroad control over the legislature.

(2) It was questionable, at least, whether the fiscal obligations imposed by the Funding Act could be met by the state if that act were accepted by all creditors. The interest on the new debt principal would just about equal the estimated revenue under the new tax law less the minimum appropriated by the constitution for public education, leaving nothing for government expenses which the auditor estimated[29] at over one million dollars. Nor was there any obvious remedy for this situation. The debt-principal was indeed reducible by sale of the state's railroad assets; but the amount receivable in the near future from this source had been rendered almost negligible by the acts noted above.[30] Expenses could be reduced only by undoing the democratic features of the constitution just put into effect; but at best this would require years. Any considerable increase in revenue depended upon economic improvement, which could come only gradually, or upon the always slow process of finding new subjects and new methods of taxation. Meantime the annual deficit would be accumu-

[29] *Report,* 1871.

[30] In 1874 only $3,400,000 had been received, Sen. *Jour.,* 1874-1875, Doc. 1. Walker's estimate (*op. cit.*) was $2,600,000 "immediately," and $10,000,000 more remotely, available.

lating so as to impair or destroy the efficiency of these proposed remedies.

(3) The "restoration of credit" policy did not rest upon a well-advised popular will. The legislature had been elected when the main issues were not fiscal. The true fiscal condition had not been made clear by the governor or by the press. While some legislators had voted from conviction for the funding and railroad acts,[31] those acts, the very backbone of the governor's policy, could scarcely have been passed without the combination of interests and the skill of lobbyists. The governor himself was known to be financially interested, directly or indirectly, in state bonds.[32] Men said, and no one took the trouble to deny the rumor, that the negroes had been bought.[33] It was not at all clear that the people would approve the funding of $13,000,000 of interest accruing mainly during war and reconstruction days and part of it compounded, and it would not be sufficient to say that this was offset by the release of Virginia from one-third of the whole debt ($16,000,000); for this one-third was generally considered West Virginia's fair proportion, and from this Virginia was already released in law and in equity.[34] Nor was it clear that in the clash bound to come between the schools and the debt, the people would side with the latter.

(4) Factions within Conservative ranks and a ten-

[31] Among the affirmative voters were A. B. Courtney, Charles Herndon, Daniel A. Grimsley, Meriwether Lewis, Wm. A. Anderson, George Walker, John A. McCaul, and M. Hanger.

[32] *Enquirer*, December 22, 1871; Massey, *Autobiography*, pp. 44 ff.

[33] For evidence see House *Jour.*, 1871-1872, pp. 31, 137, 297 ff.; *Whig, Enquirer, Dispatch*, February 14-20, 1872.

[34] C. U. Williams, *Present Financial Status of Virginia;* above, pp. 9-11 and note 38; *Enquirer*, March 28; *Whig*, March 18, 1871. It was thought at the time that, despite the previous refusal of West Virginia to treat, her new officials, being Democrats, would do so, Governor, *Message*, December 7, 1870, House *Docs.*, 1869-1870, Nos. 17 and 20.

dency toward demagogy were already appearing. The men of southwestern Virginia were almost solid against the Funding Act; and some of them were using language which questioned the validity of the debt.[35] Mahone's railroad supporters were strong and active men and Mahone himself was deemed a skilful and unscrupulous leader.[36] Against them were arrayed the governor and the interests represented by the *Enquirer* and the *Dispatch,* to which the Bourbon element was already allying itself. Already the *Whig* was seeking to array the masses against its enemies. "Are they not," it said, "working for Cameron and Scott and McClure . . . the Radical leaders of Philadelphia? . . . The demoralizing effects of Virginia gentlemen chaffing and bargaining with Radical adventurers are deplorable in the extreme. Colonel this, and Major that, and Mr. Somebody else, are seen hobnobbing with union leaguers from Pennsylvania, and aiding them in obtaining the most valuable franchises in the state . . ." Already, too, the *Whig* was predicting, no doubt unconsciously, its own future course: "Suppose this . . . [the Funding bill] becomes a law by appliances which stock-jobbers so well understand, . . . will the iniquity be patiently endured? Will it not give a handle to demagogues to agitate for repudiation of the whole?"[37]

To sum up: The legislature, elected under the circumstances narrated in the preceding chapter, endeavored to give effect to the democratic ideas embodied in the new constitution. At the same time, influenced by city

[35] See resolution of Colonel Pendleton in *Whig,* December 12, 1870.

[36] The *Enquirer* (November 4, 1871) charged that John F. Lewis, Republican, had been elected to the United States Senate through the coalition of the A. M. & O. and the Old Dominion Steamship Company; this appears probable, Letter of G. R. Gilmer, September 14, 1869, in *Mahone Papers.*

[37] March 18; November 2, 1871.

capitalistic interests and with the expectation of restoring public, and thereby private, credit, it adopted a "free" railroad policy and enacted "the Funding Act." Under the former, control as well as ownership of the railroads passed, or would pass, almost entirely into private hands. Under the Funding Act, the annual debt interest, collectable through tax-receivable coupons, almost equalled the entire revenue of the state. Accompanying results were a bitter railroad war in the legislature and a cry that the interests of the people had been sold out.

CHAPTER IV

REACTION, AND THE COURTS, 1871-1873

The legislation described in the previous chapter came before the people for review in the summer and fall of 1871. Since the scope of the referendum was limited by peculiar political conditions which continued to dominate public policies for several years, we must note here the development of party politics since the election of 1869.

It had by no means appeared certain to party leaders in the early months of 1870 just what the lines and policies of the future would be or which party would prevail.[1] Hitherto the strength of the Radicals had been the negro vote, but now men hoped, and sometimes seemed to expect, that the negroes, won to reason by fair treatment in their homes and in the legislature, would see that their interest could be best subserved by dividing their vote.[2] Instead of assuming the Republican leadership, Governor Walker had just declared his independence of all parties.[3] The older Republican

[1] *Cf. Dispatch*, July 11 (quoting Walker in New York *World*); also, October 22, 1869.

[2] *Whig*, July 5, 6; *Dispatch*, July 2, 3; *Enquirer*, July 1, 2, November 25, 1869. For recognition of the common interests of the races see *Whig*, July 7, 12; *Dispatch*, July 9, 1869. Walker thought one-fifth had voted Conservative in 1869, and that in two years one-half would be Conservatives, *op. cit.* The *Enquirer* believed the negro was rapidly learning his political interests. Amicable relations in the legislature are shown in *Whig*, January 6, 19, 20, 23, 1871—two negroes sitting "with their political associates, the Conservatives." Ku Klux operations (at no time severe) ceased in 1868, Sen. *Reports*, 42 Cong., 2 sess., no. 41, Pt. 1, p. 92.

[3] *Message*, February 8, 1870.

leaders had been discredited by defeat and the virtual abandonment of their policy by the federal administration. Hence, among the Republicans factions had developed, which warred with each other over the spoils and the treatment of ex-Confederates. On the other hand, the Conservative party, which had sprung into existence for a specific purpose, now achieved, had never received formal and authoritative organization. The future co-operation of ex-Whigs with ex-Democrats and of Bourbons with liberals was not assured.[4] West of the mountains the whites were in such overwhelming majority that they could not be expected to appreciate the problems of the "East"; and the reverse was also true. Meantime, from across the northern border was coming a call, to which some had already listened,[5] for men of ability and good standing to align themselves with the party which controlled national policies and distributed the national patronage.

Such a chaotic condition of parties gave to the Congressional campaign of 1870 a state-wide interest and importance. Early in the year the Richmond *State Journal* began, with the approval of Washington, a movement for a state convention which should rescue the Republican party from factional fights and give it leaders and policies less closely associated with events of the last four years. The movement was successful and the convention met in Richmond in September.[6] Though deploring the facility with which "our whilom true Republicans in office have forgotten and abjured

[4] Above, p. 20; *Enquirer*, November 25, 26, 1869; March 14, April 15, 16, 1871; *Whig*, August 11, 1869; January 13, 17, 1871.

[5] Examples are: Gen. W. C. Wickham, vice-president of the Chesapeake and Ohio Railway; Robert W. Hughes (below); Z. Turner, speaker of the House; Alex. Rives, federal district judge. General Mahone and the *Whig* were continually under suspicion.

[6] *Enquirer*, February 7, March 14, April 15, 16, 1870.

their pledges to Gen. Grant and Congress'' and though condemning Conservatism as a "contrivance to avoid the issues between the two great parties,'' this convention formally abandoned the party's past policy of "proscription and hate'' by pledging a "conciliatory policy'' in the selection of local officers and silence as to the test oath; while the platform's emphasis upon public education connected the party closely with what was best in its reconstruction work.[7]

To meet this move, leaders of *ante-bellum* Democracy urged that the Conservatives adopt a clear-cut and vigorous policy.[8] The non-partisan plan of 1869, they said, was operating as a cloak for time-serving Republicans and Independents. Therefore a state convention should be called which should draw strict party lines, affiliate with the national Democracy, and "fire the hearts'' of the white people. But the outspoken suspicion of old Whigs and the widespread fear of renewed federal interference upon the slightest provocation counselled caution. Accordingly no convention was called and no drawing of lines or statement of policies was attempted. Instead, those moderate men who had been elected to the legislature the year previous under the name of Conservatives met in caucus and, with the assistance of certain prominent Richmond sympathizers, appointed a new central committee. Through this committee, effective control of which was cautiously centered in Richmond, an address was issued. Ignoring national matters save for a suggestion as to economic relief, this address put forward home rule by the fittest as the para-

---

[7] *Whig, Enquirer, Dispatch,* September 27, 28, 1870; Dunning, *Essays,* pp. 233 ff. Grant was popular in the state on account of his attitude at Appomattox and in 1869.

[8] *E.g.,* the Lynchburg *News,* the *Tenth Legion Banner,* and the *Enquirer.*

mount issue, and on this platform invited and urged the co-operation of all.

At the ensuing elections, however, the liberal professions of neither party availed it anything. The whites voted mainly for Conservative candidates, but without enthusiasm; the negroes remained almost solidly Radical. The Radicals won eight of the eleven Congressmen, the Conservatives had a majority of 2,239 in the state as a whole.[9]

The indecisiveness of this campaign and the fact that state issues had not been directly involved left the problem of party lines and policies still an open one in the early months of 1871. Nor did the adjournment of the legislature clarify the situation, for on each of the two chief issues[10] before that body the Conservatives had divided about equally, while the Republicans had, as a whole, supported each side of both questions in turn. Hence, at the ensuing elections for local officials, men who claimed to be Conservatives ran independently in some places and received support from the negroes. Soon the Conservative central committee perceived its authority "measurably impaired" and the party itself "in the throes of distraction." Likewise, the Republicans were again divided into factions, carpet-baggers, backed by the bulk of the negroes, again insisting that Republican Congressmen should control the distribution of the federal patronage, scalawags opposing this.[11]

Again, therefore, the demand went up for a Conservative state convention. Not without misgivings, the

[9] *Annual Cyc.*, 1870; *Enquirer*, July 2, August 2, 5, October 7, November 11, 18; *Dispatch*, July 2, 6, August 5; *Whig*, March 8, 17, July 2, 22 (containing the address), 1870. The party plan of organization was that drawn by John B. Baldwin and adopted in 1867 (above, p. 20) slightly amended by the caucus.

[10] The railroad and the debt questions.

[11] References as in note 9.

central committee yielded, summoning the delegates to
Richmond, where its own headquarters were, and fixing
a late date for the meeting (August 30). The venture
proved a complete success. The old leaders, whom disabilities or inclination had kept in the background for six
years, now returned and were received with enthusiasm.
This was an important event, for it marked the beginning of a Confederate reaction not only against Radicalism but also against the compromising idea that had
prevailed for two years. It was, indeed, the beginning
of a "Confederate cult," the deep influence of which
was to be felt in business and social life as well as in
politics for many years to come.[12] By common consent,
issues of the Civil War period and before were laid aside
as "dead." There was no considerable expression of
Bourbon opinion on democracy and the new constitution. Despite some slight opposition on the ostensible
ground that it would give the impression of outside
dictation, an invitation to sit with the convention was
extended to Governor Walker in appreciation of his services in 1869. Six negro delegates from Richmond were
received with applause; and though bluff General Early
left in a rage, declaring that he had come thinking "this
was to be a convention of Virginia gentlemen—a white
man's convention," the Richmond press enthusiastically
described the event as "historical." As a concession to
the representative principle, a resolution offered by
H. H. Riddleberger, of the Valley, that the "consulting"
members of the central committee should be selected by
the delegates from the several Congressional districts
instead of by the convention president was adopted;
but effective party direction was left concentrated in
Richmond, and provision was made for bringing prominent local men into harmony with this management

[12] *Cf.* below, pp. 48, 109, 133.

through local reorganization on a democratic basis. Sternly refusing to consider any other question the convention put before the people the single issue of the previous year: "Conservative or Radical control?"[13]

To meet the enthusiasm created by this move, the Republicans could only develop the policy adopted the year previous. By carefully packing their convention, and obtaining the personal attendance of Washington officials, and after a long secret conference of leaders, they were able to restore party harmony. Defeat of the carpet-bagger plan for controlling federal patronage manifested unmistakably the dominance of the liberal wing. Thus the way was prepared for co-operation in the coming national elections with the many whites who did not relish an alliance with the national Democratic party. To these, and to old Whigs especially, the platform extended a cordial and liberal invitation. In state matters, the party's special interest in public education prompted a serious enquiry whether the schools, especially those for the negro, would be safe under continued Conservative control. With Conservatives in possession of the courts, the platform continued, the negro's constitutional right to serve on juries was unquestionably being destroyed; beyond doubt, the operation of the Funding Act would cause a doubling of taxes.[14]

The issue of the campaign that followed was the one

[13] *Whig*, July 20, 22, (address of state committee), 27; *Dispatch*, July 23, August 19, 23; *Enquirer, Dispatch, Whig*, August 30, 31, September 1, 1871. The change in the *Enquirer's* ownership had brought it into fairly close harmony with Governor Walker, above, p. 21. Raleigh T. Daniel as party chairman named Robert L. Montague president, and he appointed William Smith chairman of the committee on business, to which all important matters were referred. This arrangement was at once a recognition of old leaders and a necessary step in identifying the new Conservative party with the old (above, p. 20).

[14] *Whig*, January 13, 17; *Dispatch, Enquirer, Whig*, September 28, 29, 1871.

stated by the Conservatives—"Conservative or Radical rule?" Inspired by the example of their old leaders, the great bulk of the whites voted for the Conservative candidates, and the negroes for the Republican candidates, each regardless of other issues. The Conservatives, consequently, won with an increased majority in both houses.

The policy of the Conservatives, however, did not entirely prevent other issues from having weight; and herein lies a further characteristic of Virginia politics for several years to come. These issues were discussed and roughly decided by the Conservatives in each legislative district separately, and when the district was a close one, not only the regular Conservatives but also the doubtful and apathetic voters had weight. In this campaign such issues were: the public school and local government systems, the number and salary of legislators, the railroad policy, private interest rate, exemption laws, and the Funding Act. How general the discussion was can not be determined; but that it was often vigorous may be inferred from the comment frequently made that the nature of these questions and the ignorance of the voters rendered the local demagogue dangerous. Particularly noteworthy were the arguments advanced against the Funding Act: That it had been passed by the corrupt influence of brokers and speculators; that before any assumption of obligation had been agreed to there should have been a settlement with West Virginia because the debt was "created by the whole state before any division of her territory or any destruction of her property in slaves"; and that it made "the taxes of the rich payable in coupons at far less than par value, while the poor . . . [would] be compelled to pay . . . dollar for dollar." Of course such a method of deciding important questions did not yield the definite and organized expression of popular will ordinarily obtained through political parties. Thus in the present instance only twenty-six of the one hundred and thirty-two members of the previous House were returned; but the exact reasons for the change and the intentions of the new members were not at all clear.[15]

To the legislature thus elected Governor Walker reasserted his fiscal views, December 6, 1871. Reminding the members that "as a legal proposition the interest on the funded debt must unquestionably be paid," he demanded, in substance, that three-fourths of the current revenue should be used for this purpose. Referring lightly to "what may be appropriated for school purposes," he suggested as a substitute for the constitutional appropriation a poll tax of two dollars, prepayment of which should be a suffrage requisite. The governor's belief was, plainly, that if the people wanted free schools, good roads, improved asylums, an agricultural department, and the like, they would submit to higher taxes.[16]

But the legislature forthwith voted, by a majority of 119 to 33 in the two houses, that the operation of the Funding Act be suspended. This action was vetoed by the governor because it was contrary to sound public policy and discriminated against those who had not funded; and this reasoning prevailed with the Senate.[17] Thereupon a bill prohibiting the receipt of coupons for

[15] *Cf. Whig*, October 31, November 1, 10, 1871; January 2, 3, 1872; *Enquirer*, September 1, 18, November 6, 9, 1871; January 8, 1872; *Dispatch*, March 8, 1872; December 19, 1873; Ruffin, *Facts;* C. U. Williams, *Present Financial Status;* C. T. O'Ferrall, *Forty Years of Active Service*, pp. 194 ff.; *Memoirs of Governor William Smith*, p. 276; *Annual Cyc.*, 1871. Richmond Conservatives nominated and elected representatives of the German and Irish elements, *Dispatch, Whig*, September 27, 1871.

[16] Governor, *Message*, December 6, 1871; Auditor, *Report*, 1871. *Cf.* pp. 26, 29.

[17] Sen. *Jour.*, 1871-1872, pp. 88, 111; acts in force March 7, 19, 1872.

taxes was passed, notwithstanding the veto, and the payment of four per cent interest on the whole debt recognized as Virginia's was ordered. But the state supreme court, early in the next legislative session, declared by a vote of three to one that the state must receive for taxes the coupons of all bonds issued under the Funding Act prior to the attempted prohibition because they constituted a contract between the holder and the state.[18] Under this decision a preferred class of bonds, soon known as "consols," was created to the amount of some twenty millions, or about two-thirds of the whole. The legislature deemed it impracticable—as, indeed, it was— to remedy this discrimination against "peelers"[19] by making the interest on them also receivable in payment for taxes, and the holders of consols refused to surrender their privileged position.[20] The governor suggested, and the legislature adopted, a joint resolution petitioning the federal government to assume the whole debt; but the only result of this was a temporary rise in the bond market.[21]

In other respects, also, the legislature pursued a course

[18] Antoni v. Wright, 22 *Grattan*, 833, December 13, 1872. Judge Staples dissented.

[19] Strictly this term applied only to bonds issued between the passage of the prohibiting act and the court's decision; but it will be used for all bonds other than consols.

[20] Under the initiative of the legislature a conference with creditors was attempted; but its only result was a demonstration of bad feeling between legislature and creditors, *Enquirer*, February 19, 21, 22, 1873.

[21] Sen. *Jour.*, 1872-1873, December 16; joint resolution of March 26, 1873; *Whig, Dispatch, Enquirer*, February 18, 1873, and quotations in *Whig* showing division of press. For New York opinion of the stock-jobbing nature of the proposal see *Whig*, February 12, 1873, quoting New York *Advertiser*. Henry A. Wise had favored such a petition by Virginia, West Virginia, and the creditors jointly (B. H. Wise, *Henry A. Wise*, p. 397), and Governor Kemper (*Message*, January 1, 1874), endorsed it on the ground of duty incident to the war. But the plan never had influence other than that indicated above.

quite antagonistic to the restoration of credit policy. It taxed state bonds on the theory that they were private property; it ordered an investigation of the passage of the Funding Act;[22] it put bonds held by the colleges in a specially favored class;[23] and established, in the interest of farmers and local politicians, the Virginia Agricultural and Mechanical Institute;[24] it repealed the act for a general sale of the state's railroad assets; refused even to consider a somewhat similar plan for disposing of the James River and Kanawha Canal; and resumed the older policy, under which the great era of railroad consolidation and expansion was soon brought to a close.[25] It limited the permissible private interest rate to eight per cent, which was even lower than that allowed in the unamended constitution, rendered easier the redemption of lands held for delinquent taxes, and tried seriously, though in vain, to stave off the threatened defeat of the exemption laws by the state courts.[26] Aided by the general desire of the whites to be rid of an impracticable "Yankee idea," it took the first steps toward amending the local government system.[27] It

[22] House *Jour.*, 1871-1872; *Dispatch*, March, 1871, *passim; Whig*, August 8, 1877.

[23] An act of February 23, 1867, authorizing payment of full interest on their bonds was continued in force by act of March 20, 1872, and from time to time thereafter, Second Auditor, *Report*, 1879, p. 10.

[24] *Acts*, 1871-1872, pp. 48, 312. It was to be supported by the proceeds from two-thirds of the land scrip donated by Congress in 1862, and by a local appropriation; but state appropriations were of course soon made.

[25] The old railroad wars continued, however, being especially fierce in 1874 and 1875. *Cf. Dispatch, Whig, Enquirer, passim.* They ceased with the appointment of receivers for most of the roads in 1876 and 1877. *Acts*, 1871-1872, p. 45; *Annual Cyc.*, 1872, 1873; *Brown Papers.*

[26] Above; *Acts*, 1871-1872, pp. 72, 99; 1872-1873, pp. 138, 177, 329. The exemption act of June 27, 1870, and the clause of the state constitution on which it was based were declared unconstitutional by the state supreme court in 1872, 22 *Grattan*, 266.

[27] Above, p. 18.

shifted the burden of taxation noticeably from the farmer and the laborer to luxuries and corporate wealth.[28]   But it did not increase the revenues nor immediately decrease expenses.

Radical as this legislation was, it probably fell short of the popular wishes.   For of the two houses the lower was at once the "fresher from the people" and the more extreme.   Moreover, a majority of the legislators represented the upper and middle classes, the negroes and the "odds and ends" having voted for Republicans and Independents who advocated more extreme action in economic and fiscal matters.   Did the people of the state, then, wish to repudiate?   Some thought so.[29]   Certainly, the first step toward repudiating "peelers" had been taken. Yet the legislators intended only to get rid of town and corporate influences and Yankee ideas, to regain control over the state's finances so as to adjust them equitably and rationally, and to give the substantial country people a chance to recover.[30]   This was certainly a very natural course for farmers and ex-Confederates to take, and by no means an improper one.   On the announcement of the court's decision, however, most of them

[28] This was done (1) by permitting revaluation of land and the oyster catch; (2) by imposing taxes on gross receipts of transportation and insurance companies in addition to license and property taxes; (3) by a sales tax, as well as license tax, on liquor.   Not all of this was new, but the tendency was decidedly as stated.   See *Acts*, 1871-1872 (including extended session).

[29] For vote on suspension of funding, see Sen. *Jour.*, 1871-1872, p. 88; *Enquirer*, December 16, 1871; Ruffin, *Facts*.   Conservatives favoring suspension were: Thomas J. Christian, A. Fulkerson, C. T. O'Ferrall, F. McMullin, H. H. Riddleberger, Wm. R. Taliaferro, Wm. R. Terry.   On prohibiting receipt of coupons for taxes the party vote was: ayes, 81 Conservatives, 33 Republicans, 5 Independents; noes, 32 Conservatives, 1 Republican.   The vote on the private interest rate bill was quite similar.

[30] See House resolution of December 23, 1871; *Whig*, December 28, 29; *contra*, *Enquirer*, December 20, 1871; *Religious Herald* and *Central Presbyterian*, in *Enquirer*, February 19, 1872.

yielded out of traditional respect; and it was they who blocked further action of the same character. But Republicans and Independents and a minority of the Conservatives, chiefly those from the "Southwest," agreed with the dissenting judge[31] that the decision was wrong in law because under it "liens and mortgages may be given upon the future revenues of the state, by statutes assuming the form of contracts"; and with the *Whig*[32] that it substantiated an impression begun since the war that "the law which is dispensed is wanting in the essential elements of justice and equity."

Thus, by 1872, party lines and policies had become definitely established. Despite its varied program of liberalism, democracy, and reform, the Republican party was controlled, through federal appointees, from Washington, and few besides the negroes were attracted to it. On the other hand, the Conservative party relied upon its single promise of native white control; and this sufficed both to hold together the Bourbons and the capitalistic interests and to control the state legislature. The elections of 1871, however, had disclosed a wide difference of opinion among Conservatives, due in part to a Confederate reaction, now just beginning, and in part to divergence of economic and social interests and principles. Especially noteworthy was the legislature's attack upon the Funding Act. This subsided, however, when the attempts at undoing the act met defeats at the hands of the governor and the courts. But the Richmond *Whig* and other Conservatives, especially in the "Southwest," bitterly condemned governor and courts as well as the Funding Act. Republicans shared this hostility.

[31] Judge Staples lived in the "Southwest."
[32] December 17, 18, 1872.

CHAPTER V

"DEBT PAYERS," AND THE ELEMENTS OF DISSATISFACTION, 1874-1877

As the campaigns of 1870 and 1871 fixed unalterably the issue between the Conservatives and the Radicals, so the contest for governor and legislature in 1873 and the events growing immediately out of it sealed the fate of the Republican party until its rejuvenation in the early eighties.[1]

The prospects of the Republicans at the beginning of the campaign were bright. Through their victory over the Conservatives supporting the Liberal-Democratic combination headed by Greeley the year previous, they were enabled to urge with more effect than before the futility of the non-partisan idea. Though the Conservatives quite correctly attributed this defeat to their candidate and not to their party policy, they could conceal neither their factions nor the failure of their fiscal efforts; and so good a politician as Governor Walker declared confidentially that only two Conservatives could be sure of carrying the state that year (1873).[2] Accordingly, being assured of continued support from the federal administration, liberal Republican leaders early took the initiative and by July were able to assemble a state convention marked, as in 1871, by the domination of federal employees and the subordination

[1] See ch. 13.
[2] Letter to W. H. Ruffner, May 7, *Ruffner Papers*. Walker's view, however, proved incorrect. Walker was now recognized as a Conservative.

of the negroes. For governor they nominated Robert W. Hughes, once an extreme secessionist but now federal district-attorney in the "Southwest," a man of excellent family, the "brains of his party," and a reputed favorite of Grant. Carpet-baggers were represented by C. P. Ramsdell, of Surry, and old Union men by David Fultz, of the once strongly Whiggish county of Augusta. In an intelligent and well written platform they offered to the "Southwest" development of its resources through outside capital and federal aid; to the railroads, a "free" policy; and to liberal sentiment, the hospitable reception of immigrants, exact and impartial justice, and fair elections. As in 1872, they endorsed the administration of the schools under Supt. William H. Ruffner,[3] Conservative though he was, urging only a more democratic method of selecting the local trustees. Shifting to meet the changed situation, they condemned repudiation in any form and promised compulsory adjustment with West Virginia through use of the federal courts.[4]

The Conservatives, however, again refused to recognize any issue save negro rule under federal direction. Their newspapers refrained from expressing gubernatorial preferences, and their convention, marked even more than in 1871 by the prominence of old leaders, spent its energies in stately compliments to itself and bitter denunciation of Radicalism. A brief platform noted the results of Radical rule in the Southern states, declared for "exact and impartial justice" to both races, pointed "with pride" to the school system, promised to co-operate with "Gen. Grant" in cultivating good will between the sections, and urged the completion of the James River and Kanawha Canal as a matter of national

[3] Below, p. 60.
[4] *Enquirer, Whig,* July 31, August 1; *Dispatch,* August 7, 1873; *Annual Cyc.,* 1873.

importance. For governor they named Gen. James L. Kemper, of the Valley, a soldier of two wars and twice Speaker, a liberal in politics and a friend of Mahone in the railroad war. Then, by a dramatic *coup*, they compelled Kemper's closest competitor, Col. R. E. Withers (now of the "Southwest"), an ex-Bourbon and an enemy of Mahone, to accept the second place. The ticket was completed with the name of Raleigh T. Daniel, of Richmond, a lawyer and editor of war-time fame and since the war the dominating party chairman.[5] Likewise, in the campaign that followed, the Conservatives permitted but one issue; with this they colored all the brilliant liberal speeches of Hughes. Hitherto they had carefully refused to draw the race line; now, without nominally changing this policy, they refused in places to enter joint discussions and by thus "dividing the crowd" compelled white men to support the Conservative party or repudiate their color. After this the result was never in doubt. Hughes was overwhelmingly defeated.[6]

The Republican party now began to pay in full for the indignities which it had attempted to heap upon ex-Confederates. For some time trickery and fraud had been practiced by the Conservatives and the drawing of the color line tended to encourage the practice. But such methods were ever uncertain in their results, they lacked social respectability and were in direct defiance of stat-

[5] Above, pp. 20, 30. The chairmanship of the state committee and that of the executive committee were hereafter held by different men.

[6] *Dispatch*, July 13, August 8, November 4, 5; *Enquirer*, July 18, 20, August 7, 8; *Whig*, July 17, August 5. 7, 8; November 4, 5, 12, 1873; Withers, *Autobiography*, p. 313. For Mahone's share in the selection of Kemper, see below, p. 70. That Republicans hoped for assistance from public school men is indicated by a letter of Hughes to Superintendent Ruffner, April 24, 1873, and by the reported assertion of Ramsdell that Superintendent Ruffner was not in accord with Conservative policy as to schools; also by the preparation of John W. Daniel (letter to Ruffner, October 1, 1873), to meet the move, *Ruffner Papers*.

utes which their sponsors had made.[7] So an amendment
to the suffrage law embedded in the constitution was proposed by the legislature in 1874 and ratified in 1876,
under which failure to pay the poll tax and conviction
for many petty crimes became disqualifications. This
limitation of suffrage, together with the abolition of one-
third of the local offices, was an "undoing of reconstruction" which rendered unnecessary the constitutional convention that would otherwise probably have been called.[8]
As a result, the hold of Republicans, already weakened
in the counties and towns, was now broken completely.
Of the two federal senators chosen by the compromising
legislature of 1869, one had proved to be a good Conservative and the other was replaced by Colonel Withers
in 1875; next year the Conservatives elected all but one
of the members of the House.[9] By the end of Kemper's
administration (1878), therefore, federal appointees had
become not only the dominating leaders of the Republican party but almost the party itself. With this condition of affairs they appeared quite content.

When Governor Kemper began his term, January 1,
1874, Virginia faced not only the effects of a far-reaching
national panic—in her case unrelieved by previous prosperity—but also the fiscal woes inevitably arising from

[7] Knight v. Johnson, Sen. *Jour.*, 1875-1876, Doc. 3; Platt v. Goode, in
C. H. Rowell, *Digest of Contested Election Cases; Acts*, May 11, 1870;
March 30, 1871; April 30, 1874

[8] *Thorpe*, 3901, above, pp. 19, 44. A. E. McKinley in "Two Southern
Constitutions" (*Political Science Quarterly*, IX, p. 671) quite overlooks
this fact. The bulking of the negroes made such laws necessary. The
political motive is evident from the fact that negroes voted against them.
Cf. Dunning, "Undoing of Reconstruction, in *Atlantic Monthly*,
LXXXVIII, p. 437.

[9] In 1874 and in 1876 ex-Governor Walker was chosen by Conservatives
of the Richmond district, previously represented by the Radicals C. H.
Porter and James A. Smith. At the expiration of his second term he
returned to New York.

previous policies. The legislature of 1870-1871 had avoided the problem of current debt interest by permitting the greater part of it to be funded. The succeeding legislature had managed to retard the annual million dollar inflow of coupons by offering four per cent in cash and two per cent certificates in exchange for them, while making their sale for tax-paying purposes difficult.[10] By means of these devices and the habitual under-payment of appropriations for other purposes, especially for the "peeler" debt, the annual deficit of about a million dollars had been temporarily concealed.[11] But now the large surplus which had existed at the beginning of Governor Walker's administration was gone. Nearly a million dollars in authorized cash payments and half a million in tax-receivable coupons were outstanding, the current year would show a deficit of almost another million, the bulk of the state's assets had been bargained away, and general economic conditions demanded a decrease, rather than an increase, in taxes.[12]

The fiscal views of the new governor were unknown at the time of his election, the debt not having been a campaign issue that year. To the great disgust of the financial world, however, he attacked the problem at once, somewhat after the manner of the legislature of 1871-1872. The fundamental need, he said, was a "permanent financial policy." The first essential of this policy was equality of creditors and uniformity of obligations, and the proper way to obtain these objects was

[10] Acts of March 19, 1872 (repealed December 23, 1872); March 13, 1873; December 24, 1872 (prohibiting collecting officers from dealing in coupons and imposing a broker's license tax on other persons dealing in them). Only some $300,000 in coupons were turned in for taxes up to October 1, 1873, Second Auditor, *Report*, 1873.

[11] *Message*, March 8, 1870.

[12] Auditor, *Report*, 1874. In addition there were $1,800,000 of deferred interest certificates.

to call a conference of consol holders and induce them to exchange their tax-receivable coupons for, say, four per cent in cash and two per cent in deferred interest certificates. The second essential was prompt payment of interest, for which the necessary money could be obtained only by a more careful administration of the revenue laws, by finding new subjects of taxation, and by reducing expenses in proportion to the state's reduced capacity, through a constitutional convention if necessary.[13]

The legislature endorsed the governor's proposal by authorizing the conference, and named the governor and R. M. T. Hunter, the treasurer, as the state's representatives. At the appointed time, ex-Secretary of the Treasury Hugh McCulloch came to represent part of the British holders; Richmond men and some members of the legislature spoke for most of the other creditors. In a long address the governor portrayed the extreme distress of the people and the heaviness of the state's burdens, coupling with this gloomy picture a severe arraignment of his predecessor for misrepresentation of the facts and waste of the state's assets. Asserting that there was a strong sentiment against the debt entertained by "leading minds," he intimated that the coupons could be successfully fought. On the other hand, he emphasized the desire of the state to be perfectly fair and her ability to meet her obligations if given time for recovery. The creditors' representatives agreed with the governor that the state could pay four per cent now and should soon be able to pay six per cent. They could do no more, however, than resolve that if punctual payment of interest should be guaranteed, those consol holders who had no taxes to pay would, in their opinion, accept the terms

---

[13] *Messages,* January 1, March 27 (Sen. *Jour.,* 1874, Doc. 17), December 2, 1874 (with appended speech before the conference, Sen. *Jour.,* 1874-1875, Doc. 1).

proposed by the governor.[14] Out of this resolution grew several propositions, more or less authorized, for funding the consol debt. But from the stringency of their terms it was obvious that the holders of consols intended to surrender their position of preferred creditors only for a better one, and that they would permit no relief to holders of "peelers." This attitude they soon made very clear by thrusting upon the treasury a deluge of coupons.[15]

Thus by 1875 two attempts at undoing the Funding Act had been undertaken by the Conservatives, and had failed. Further agitation would probably prove equally futile. It might injure the party; it would handicap business, already sorely distressed and clamoring for a cessation of attacks upon credit, and it would be accompanied by appeals to the whims and passions of the masses, to which the Bourbons, now rapidly recovering their old-time influence, were bitterly opposed. Accordingly, in the opinion of a majority of the legislature and of almost the entire press, nothing remained but to "pay the debt." This view Governor Kemper accepted. And with his acceptance began a united and truly heroic attempt on the part of almost all the upper classes to meet the state's obligations as they stood.

The program of the "debt payers" was divided into three parts: reduction of expenses, increase of revenues, and reorganization of the sinking fund.

14 *Op. cit.; Dispatch*, November 11, 1874. Senator H. W. Thomas, of Alexandria, presided; James Dooley, of Richmond, was secretary. Seventy-five to eighty per cent of the consols were held outside the state. Below, p. 89.

15 Sen. *Jour.*, 1874-1875, Doc. 4; *Dispatch*, November II, 18, 1874; Second Auditor, *Report*, 1875. The *Dispatch* (December 18, 1876) advocated a waiting attitude. The *Enquirer* (December 12) believed the whole attempt "a lame demagogic movement." Even the *Whig* (December 3) was unenthusiastic.

State expenses[16] for all "ordinary" purposes from
1850 to 1860, according to Governor Kemper, averaged
$588,236; from 1869 to 1875, $1,084,189—an increase of
eighty-four per cent with population and territory
reduced nearly one-third. Among "extraordinary"
expenses, also, there were new and increased items (quite
apart from the public debt) the total of which is not
easily ascertainable. Some of these items were due to
inefficiency and petty graft, often concealed in fees,
travelling expenses, and the like. Others, however, were
the unavoidable outcome of war and reconstruction.
Such were the one hundred and twenty-five per cent
increase in "criminal expenses" for which emancipation
and the cumbersome judicial system were responsible,
and the eighty-seven per cent in legislative costs for
which matters of race adjustment, the unprecedented
fiscal situation, and the enlarged powers and duties of
the General Assembly offered sufficient reason. Such,
too, were increases of some $275,000 for public schools
and of perhaps $50,000 for the care of lunatics, a class of
expenses which popular approval quite as much as positive law rendered unavoidable.[17] This situation the

16 Local expenses were curtailed through reducing township officers from
twelve to eight and giving the legislature control over local debts. *Cf.*
above, p. 50.

17 Governor, *Message,* December 1, 1875; Sen. *Jour.,* 1859-1860, Doc. 33;
Annual Reports, 1877; "Civis" (B. Puryear, professor in Richmond College) in *Religious Herald,* January 17 to February 28, 1878. The division
between "ordinary" and "extraordinary" expenses is largely an arbitrary
one; but the comparison made by Kemper appears fair. "Criminal
expenses" were allowances made by the state to the county and circuit
courts; the penitentiary was an additional expense, the negroes furnishing
the great bulk of the inmates. In 1879, 110 lunatics were being kept in
jail and other places besides asylums at an expense to the state of $35,000
a year. Emancipation both increased the amount of crime and transferred the policing of the negro from private to public hands; so with
lunacy. An illustration of pettiness appears in Sen. *Jour.,* 1877-1878,
Doc. 12, where it is reported that of $1,300 appropriated for the encourage-

"debt payers" attacked vigorously, some favoring a return to the standard of 1860 or perhaps even lowering it in proportion to war losses.[18] But the Radicals, insisting that the adoption of more direct penalties and more summary processes would degrade the lower classes, retarded the adoption of a revised criminal code until 1879; then an annual saving of $50,000 was at once shown. Though the legislature as early as 1874 proposed a constitutional amendment reducing its own membership and substituting biennial for annual sessions, this amendment did not become effective until 1880, because, some said, legislators liked Richmond and their easy salaries. Though both Walker and Kemper had earnestly urged more work and fewer clerks in the departmental offices, every effort in this direction was blocked by the "associated influence" of interested persons.[19] There seemed, indeed, to be two fundamental difficulties. The leaders insisted upon treating alike, as equally foreign and objectionable, those expenses which were mere abuses and those which in the long run would prove both popular and productive. Again, some fees and salaries had come to be considered the customary reward of politicians, great and small, and necessary, in the absence of federal patronage, to keep the state out of the hands of the negroes. The result was that a standard of econ-

ment of immigration, $1,000 went for a *Summary of Virginia*, of which libraries received 303 copies, legislators 1,760, and 43 were sold. Half the legislature's time was consumed in private legislation, sometimes for minor matters—empowering a high school to grant certificates of distinction, for example.

[18] Above, p. 20; "Civis," *op. cit.*

[19] *Acts*, 1877-1878, p. 207; *Thorpe*, VII, 3903; Sen. *Jour.*, 1877-1878, Doc. 7; Auditor, *Reports;* Governor, *Message*, December 1, 1877; "Civis," *op. cit.* Under the revised code the first to suffer the penalty of whipping was a white man in Norfolk, and at the hands of a negro constable, *Annual Cyc.*, 1878.

omy severe even to niggardliness[20] was set for new
undertakings without effecting any considerable elimination of abuses or curtailment of expenses.

The tax-paying class believed themselves to be getting
poorer. In 1875, though the full effects of neither the
long period of depreciating prices nor the panic of 1873
had yet been felt, reassessment of realty showed a loss
of twelve per cent as compared with 1870.[21] Unused to
heavy taxes the people believed their burdens already
too great. Every year $7,000,000 of excise taxes were
collected in the state, and, on a per capita basis, the
state's share of the tariff amounted to nearly $6,000,000;
these great sums, the tax-paying class believed, were
paid by the people of the state. Besides, state and local
taxes amounted to over $5,000,000.[22] To increase the
state's revenues was, accordingly, very difficult. Treasurer R. M. T. Hunter devised a tax revision scheme
intended primarily to reach personalty; but, as such a
scheme would affect landowners primarily, it was quietly
dropped, for opinion was all but unanimous that the landowners could stand no further burden. Taxes on business licenses were tried as far as the increasing political
importance of the merchant and the doctor permitted.[23]
Capital, notwithstanding its demand for an honest debt
policy, availed itself of every constitutional safeguard,
of old charter exemptions, and of the strong railroad
contingent in the legislature; not until 1879 did it pay

[20] Below, pp. 59 ff. Because of poverty the state was not represented at
the Centennial Exposition.

[21] Act of March 31, 1875; Auditor, *Reports*, 1871, Doc. 9; *ibid.*, 1877,
Doc. 7. The valuations were $279,000,000 and $246,000,000 (currency).

[22] Sen. *Jour.*, 1874-1875, Doc. 1.

[23] See, for example, tax bill of 1874. In 1879, these yielded (exclusive
of licenses to manufacture and sell liquor) $340,000—a very great increase
over 1871.

as much as $120,000.[24] Great efforts were made to reach the masses. Thus a dog tax, it was urged, would net large sums; but the legislature gave it only a brief and imperfect trial, for the dogs' owners had votes.[25] For a similar reason the suggested increase of the poll tax from one dollar to two was not tried; and the requirement that the dollar tax be paid before voting netted little additional revenue.[26] Dr. Moffett, of the Valley, fathered an act for taxing the consumption of liquor which was expected to produce half a million and to solve the whole matter. But the liquor dealers, now an important political factor, fought it so successfully that there was a large loss the first year, only a slight gain the second, and in the third the act was repealed.[27]

At the beginning of Kemper's administration the state had two sinking funds: one amounting to a million and a half dollars in 1861, but dormant since then; the other created by the act of March 31, 1871, for the reception of proceeds from the public works. Both were invested almost entirely in state bonds. By an act of March 31, 1875, the former fund was revived and consolidated with the latter, and payment of interest on the whole was authorized. The practice immediately arose of investing this interest in the cheaper state securities. This practice was open to the serious objection that the state was paying herself interest in preference to her creditors, and was depreciating their holdings in order to buy them in at a low price. But it

[24] For efforts and difficulties see tax bill of 1871-1872 (extended session); act of February 4, 1873; Governor, *Message,* December 3, 1879; Auditor, *Reports, passim.*

[25] *Acts,* 1871-1872; 1872-1873; *Whig,* January 3, 20, 1877.

[26] Below.

[27] *Acts,* 1876-1877, pp. 245, 301; 1878-1879, p. 310; 1879-1880, p. 147; Auditor, *Reports; Enquirer,* March 3, April 1; *Dispatch,* February 7, 1877; January 17, 1879. The motive appears to have been mainly fiscal. Regulation of the business was quite a problem, however, *Whig,* January 5, 1879.

was certainly legal because the constitution required a sinking fund, and it was probably just because it provided a market for peelers at a time when funds were not available for interest on them.[28] Moreover, it seemed to assure their eventual retirement. By 1877 the total of this fund was $5,145,271; by 1879, $5,841,620.[29]

By 1877 in the opinion of Governor Kemper,[30] the fiscal results of these efforts were very encouraging. For the fiscal year 1876-1877, Kemper estimated a net gain of nearly $200,000 over the average for eight years. "It is as clear as a mathematical demonstration," he wrote, "that, if the legislature shall leave the general features of the present revenue system untouched . . . , the current resources of the treasury will hereafter suffice to pay full interest on the entire outstanding debt." But this optimism, so characteristic of debt payers, found little warrant in the auditor's reports of that year. Over four millions of interest were accrued and unpaid on July 1. Presuming an increase of $125,000 in revenues the next year, the annual deficit would still be $600,000.

But this policy of the debt payers, commendable as it

[28] Authorization of four per cent cash (and a two per cent certificate) for interest on the funded and two-thirds the unfunded was made in 1874 and 1878, provided so much could be spared. In 1876, in order to avoid the discussion always occasioned by special authorizations, interest payment was left entirely to the auditor's discretion under the last clause of the general appropriation act, *Acts,* 1874, p. 264; 1874-1875, p. 366; 1875-1876, p. 263. The amount actually paid in cash in 1876 was $158,000, and in 1877, $68,000, Auditor, *Report,* 1876, Doc. 3; *ibid.,* 1877, Doc. 4.

[29] See C. U. Williams, *Present Financial Status of Virginia.* Apparently, in 1879 some $2,000,000 represented the old fund and its invested interest; some $50,000, the bonds of defaulting officials; $1,540,000 had been ''purchased by the commissioners'' apparently under act of March 31, 1875; and the rest had come from the sales of state assets. See Second Auditor, *Report,* 1873, Doc. C.

[30] *Message,* December 5, 1877. Compare with message of December 6, 1876, for the governor's optimism.

was, contained one serious defect. It did not take into account the elements of dissatisfaction. Three illustrations of this will suffice.

Early as 1873 the farmers had begun to organize in "granges," for the purpose of alleviating the "languishing condition of agricultural interests" "caused in part by the oppression of unequal legislation, both state and national." Strongly opposed at first because they "introduced innovations upon long and well established usages of society" and endangered the Conservative party, these granges by January, 1876, numbered 685 with a membership of 18,783, including many conservative farmers and shrewd politicians. In state meetings, they appointed committees to obtain favorable legislation on transportation, immigration, and the inspection of tobacco and fertilizers. Locally, they attempted to manufacture fertilizers and to do away with the middleman's profits through co-operative stores and agencies. In 1877, however, the legislature had done little for them, the co-operative undertakings were failing, and the membership appeared to be deteriorating, with a consequent passing of leadership into more radical hands.[31]

[31] State Grange, *Proceedings*, 1874, 1876; *Southern Planter and Farmer*, 1872-1876; "Personal Recollection." The long established State Agricultural Society still existed; also local farmers' clubs. Prominent first members were J. W. White, William Taylor, and Lewis E. Harvie. In 1875, M. W. Hazlewood of Richmond (below) became secretary. Other active members were Franklin Stearns, W. H. Mann, C. T. Sutherlin, B. B. Douglass, Mann Page, J. M. Blanton, R. R. Farr (below), Wm. Ambler, Frank G. Ruffin (below). The *Virginia Patron* became the organ of the order. The *Southern Planter* was favorable, but appears never to have endorsed agitation of railroad rates. The promotion of public education was one of its declared objects, but this was not emphasized. Possibly the long and short haul law (*Acts*, 1874-1875, p. 443) procured a reduction of freight charges on grain; but the rates on guano, agricultural lime, etc., were very high and unequal, Sen. *Jour.*, 1878-1879, Doc. 19; Railroad Commissioner, *Report*, 1878. *Cf.* Magruder, *Recent Administration*, ch. 6.

To a majority of the upper classes between 1865 and 1870 the idea of a state system of public education was distinctly objectionable. The institution, they declared, was a foreign one which their conquerors sought to force upon them. Its main purpose was to break down all social ranks and put the negro upon a plane of equality with the whites. It was an experiment too costly to be tried in the impoverished condition of the state. Others, however, ignoring its immediate origin, declared the institution theoretically good and practically a necessity, in view of the breaking down of the old system and the impossibility of fitting it to the negro even if it should be revived. As a sort of compromise between these two views, it had come to be generally agreed by 1869-1871 that since the constitution had been accepted with the provision for schools in it, the experiment ought to be made in good faith. Such was the view of Governor Walker, of Gen. R. E. Lee (then president of Washington College), of the *Whig,* and probably of the *Dispatch.* To this sentiment the legislature of 1870 responded by entrusting the drafting of the school laws and, virtually, the selection of local school officials to the state superintendent, and by electing as state superintendent Rev. Dr. William Henry Ruffner, son of the famous Henry Ruffner,[32] a man of broad intelligence, marked administrative ability, and indomitable energy. Thus at once the schools were removed from the influence of ordinary politics and the foundation was laid for a system surprisingly good and destined rapidly to increase in popularity. Poverty helped; for many a genteel lady and disabled veteran found employment in the schools and threw about them a much-needed atmosphere of respectability. From the first the negroes favored them solidly. The attempted passage in 1874 of Sumner's

[32] See *Branch Historical Papers,* June, 1910.

Civil Rights Bill requiring mixed schools threatened for a moment to put them out of existence; but this was soon forgotten.[33] And though the whites generally thought that the negro's education ought to be paid for by the federal government and a request to that effect was made, still the negro received, on the whole, a reasonable share of the facilities provided.[34] By 1877 nine-tenths of the families of the state were public school patrons, and it was accounted political death for a public man to oppose openly this institution "of the people."[35]

But there still remained lurking in the financial situation a serious danger to the schools. At first, landowners had protested against the ten cent tax imposed by the state and the still larger taxes imposed by the local governments. Appreciating the importance of this landowning class, Superintendent Ruffner at once suggested the substitution of an increased poll tax and a tax on dogs and the consumption of liquor, arguing that many would contribute for schools in this manner though they would not for anything else. The suggested change was not made, but with the increased use of the schools opposition of this character gradually died away, save for the fitful attacks of that old-fashioned organ of the

[33] Rhodes, *History of the United States*, VII, 90; State Superintendent, *Report*, 1874. The legislature protested, Poore, *Descriptive Catalogue*, p. 989.

[34] The whites constituting seven-twelfths of the population (according to the census of 1880) received three-fourths of the school funds. But the negroes paid almost no taxes, were more compactly settled. Besides, it was almost impossible to get suitable teachers in sufficient numbers. For aid to the Hampton Normal and Agricultural Institute see acts of February 7, March 19, 1872.

[35] State Superintendent, *Reports*, 1871-1878; *Educational Journal of Virginia*, 1869, 1870; September, 1878; *Dispatch*, July 10, 1877; February 1, 14, 1878. Very effective in harmonizing public sentiment and the new system was the work of the *Educational Journal* of Virginia, of which John B. Minor, of the University of Virginia, was the father, and C. H. Winston, of Richmond College, the chief editor.

farmers who could not change, the *Southern Planter*. Between the schools and the debt, however, the clash grew sharper and sharper. Early as 1873[36] the superintendent, with characteristic foresight, secured the passage of an act requiring the auditor to pay the schools their constitutional quota of state funds in *cash*. Despite this it was discovered in 1876 that there was due the schools down to 1875 nearly $400,000. By 1877 this sum had increased to $526,000, and in September of the next year appeared to be $850,000. If to this amount was added the interest due on the state bonds held by the literary fund, the total "diverted" was over a million.[37] The auditor's excuse was the confusion of the state's bookkeeping and the inadequacy of the revenues. He had, he said, paid the schools more than their *pro rata* share (one-fifth) of the cash received; the government must go on; the obligation to pay the debt was equally as sacred as the schools. Worse still, from the viewpoint of school partisans, the colleges and the religious press, being habitually conservative and tied up in interest with the bond-holding class, urged the moral obligation to pay the debt while speaking of the education of the masses as a luxury.[38] Bourbons took courage, and began to talk of abolishing the new system in favor of the old one. And a prominent debt payer was understood to have said publicly that it would be better to burn the schoolhouses than to permit the state to default in interest payment on the debt. Thus it came about that, while the people were paying the school tax

[36] Act of March 29.

[37] Superintendent, *Reports*, 1876, 1877, 1878; Auditor, *Report*, 1878. Of $8,511,943 cash received by the state from 1873 to 1877, $1,912,266 was paid to the schools.

[38] Second Auditor, *Report*, 1879; *Religious Herald*, 1878, 1879, *passim*. Not all college men agreed with the auditor, *e.g.*, John B. Minor, letter to Ruffner, November 21, 1877, in *Ruffner Papers*.

and the system was growing in popularity, teachers were going unpaid and schools were closing. These facts the state superintendent did not fail to point out, and the politicians, great and small, took notice.[39]

In later years when the "Readjuster" political party had been formed,[40] certain men were often spoken of as "original readjusters." By this it was meant that they had at an early date objected to recognizing the whole debt of the state as valid, and had insisted that it be "re-adjusted." Hints of this view we have met from time to time. It originated, apparently, in a feeling of humiliation and resentment that men who had inflicted loss upon the state, and such Virginians as were now willing to ally themselves with them, should be able to levy tribute upon those who had defended her with their all. The enactment of laws staying the collection of private debts, the setting aside of a share of the public debt for West Virginia, the iniquities of the Funding Act, and the obvious impossibility of meeting its terms, all contributed to emphasize the idea in thoughtful minds.[41]

In the legislature the notable advocates of this view were Massey and Fulkerson,[42] J. Horace Lacy, of Spottsylvania, Moffett, of Rockingham, and Lybrook, of Patrick. They argued[43] that Virginia had been "con-

[39] The situation as to asylums and other public charities was similar to that of the schools. The *Enquirer* (February 4, 1875) estimated the number of the insane unprovided for at 500.

[40] Below, ch. 8.

[41] Above, *passim.*

[42] Below, p. 105.

[43] This is a composite argument. For development of Massey's views compare his letter of 1873, his speech in the House in February, 1875, his pamphlet, *Debts and Taxes,* published in the fall of 1875, and articles in the Staunton *Spectator* in 1877. The speech is in *Virginia Political Pamphlets,* I (Virginia State Library), the others in his "Autobiography." See also Ruffin, *Scrap-Book,* I (Virginia State Library), *An Appeal;* Fulkerson in *Whig,* January 13, 1879.

quered territory'' and therefore, according to the law of nations, her *ante-bellum* debts devolved upon her conqueror. If the federal government would not admit this, then equity demanded that the debt should be reduced in proportion to the impairment of the security on which it had been based—one-third for the loss of West Virginia and one-third for property destroyed by war, leaving $15,000,000 principal and interest as of 1865. No recognition of the debt was valid which had been made between 1865 and 1870, because the state was not then in possession of her ''sovereignty.'' As for the Funding Act, its moral force was vitiated by fraud in its passage; and though the courts had declared it binding, that decision was wrong in principle because it ''bound the state's sovereignty,'' and so could justifiably be reversed or avoided. The ''state's honor'' and ''restoration of credit'' arguments relied upon by debt payers were alike purely commercial. Both depended upon ability and ability was conditioned by the size of the debt. In this debt, under existing arrangements, was probably included the portion which had been pretendedly set aside for West Virginia but which was known on the market as ''Virginia deferred.''. In it certainly should be included the literary and sinking funds. Taxes on ''dogs and whiskey'' and all the painful expedients of debt payers they thought simply absurd.

After the failure of the compromise move in 1874, something like a concerted attack on coupons and a campaign for publicity had been begun under the lead of these men. Through the columns of the *Whig,* Col. Frank G. Ruffin replied in his striking style to the Council of Foreign Bondholders, London, over the signature of ''A Virginia Farmer.''[44] Massey sought to have the legislature ask explicit instructions from the

[44] Ruffin, *Scrap-Book,* I.

people as to the terms on which they were willing to compromise with creditors, and in a pamphlet known as "Debts and Taxes" he reprinted his peculiar views previously expressed through the local press.[45] In the legislature, Fulkerson, hoping to bring the Funding Act again before the courts, pushed through the House a bill imposing a tax of twenty-five per cent on coupons,[46] while Massey sought, under guise of protecting the treasury from fraud, to hamper their receipt for taxes.[47] In 1876-1877 similar efforts again met defeat; but the effects of the agitation were seen in resolutions deliberately designed to scale the debt one-half or two-thirds, which were offered by the Independent Stovall and the Radical Curlett.[48] More immediately important were the earnest efforts of careful leaders of the old school, such as R. M. T. Hunter and A. H. H. Stuart, to effect a compromise with creditors;[49] for these men, though far from accepting "original readjuster" principles, inevitably lent an atmosphere of seriousness to the idea of readjustment.

These measures had received support from practically all Republicans, Independents, and "Southwest" Conservatives, from part of the Valley Conservatives, and from individuals and counties here and there with whom times were hard.[50] There was a certain resemblance,

[45] See House resolution, in *Virginia Political Pamphlets*, I; Massey, "Autobiography."

[46] *Enquirer*, March 14, 17; *Dispatch*, March 18, 20, 1875.

[47] *Virginia Political Pamphlets*, I; *Enquirer*, February 11, 1875. Conditions warranted suspicion, see below, p. 62.

[48] House, *Jour.*, 1876-1877, index.

[49] Stuart's effort had the endorsement of William Cullen Bryant, Thurlow Weed, and Peter Cooper, but it netted only a report on war losses, *Whig*, January 11, 13; March 30, 1877. For Hunter see Ruffin, *Scrap-Book*, I.

[50] House vote on Fulkerson's proposal: "Ayes," 21 Radicals, 36 Conservatives, 1 Independent; "Noes," 3 Radicals, 41 Conservatives, 3 Independents (*Dispatch* classification, March 18, 1875). Among Valley

taking them as a group, between these men and Mahone's railroad faction, though the two were by no means identical. They were friendly to the schools. Some of them were prominent in the granges. They had back of them, however, no organization, no strong press support,[51] no great financial interests. At the beginning of 1877 it seemed that this second wave of repudiation, like that of 1867-1868, had been completely beaten off by the determination and influence of "debt payers."

Summarizing, we find that though the Republicans won the national elections of 1870 and 1872, their party was again beaten in the state elections in 1873, and thereafter rapidly declined. This result was due in part to the Confederate reaction and in part to restrictive legislation. In this legislation the influence of Bourbonism, as well as that of politics, was reflected. The fiscal situation had now become acute. Accordingly, when creditors had refused to compromise despite veiled threats from the new governor, Conservative leaders informally adopted a policy of "paying the debt" through decreasing expenses, increasing revenues, and redeeming the cheaper bonds. This policy completed the union between Bourbons and the city capitalistic interests. But, though faithfully pursued for four years, it met only partial success owing at once to depressed economic conditions and to the burden unavoidably imposed by emancipation and the new constitution. Moreover, such a policy involved no attempt at conciliation of the farmers, now seeking defence of their interests

members not voting was Riddleberger. Ross Hamilton (below) and James B. Richmond voted "aye," Lybrook and Allen (below) voted "no." Examples of counties probably influenced by hard times are Spottsylvania, Stafford, Lancaster, and Essex.

[51] The *Whig* favored compromise, but not Massey's and Fulkerson's methods.

in the granges, nor did it appease school partisans to see "debt payers" and Bourbons united against them. Believing all other remedies futile, "original read-justers" now openly began not only to demand that the debt be scaled but also to fight the tax-receivable coupons in the legislature and the public press with a view to forcing the issue.

CHAPTER VI

MAHONE AND THE BARBOUR BILL, 1877-1878

Both governor and legislature were to be chosen in 1877. At last, owing to Republican disorganization and apathy,[1] the Conservatives were free to act without the restraining fear of Radical domination. But it was impossible at once to break the habit of years, and the habit had been to refer all issues, save that of race control, to the decision of the legislative districts, and to follow in these districts the leadership of war heroes.[2] Personal and sectional rivalries, therefore, rather than economic and social issues, characterized the gubernatorial race in its earlier stages. The "Southwest" presented Gen. William Terry; the Valley, Colonel Holliday;[3] the Piedmont, Maj. John W. Daniel; the Tidewater, Gen. William B. Taliaferro; while Gen. Fitzhugh Lee's friends urged him as a compromise candidate. None of these expressed, or was expected to express, opinions on the burning economic and social questions of the day, for the convention must be left free to "point with pride," as of old. From this negative attitude the campaign was rescued by the candidacy of General Mahone.

William Mahone[4] was essentially a self-made man.

[1] Above, p. 50; below, p. 134.

[2] See above, p. 48.

[3] F. W. M. Holliday was born in Winchester. He studied at Yale and later took a law course at the University of Virginia.

[4] W. L. Royall, *Some Reminiscences;* Withers, *Autobiography;* O'Ferrall, *Forty Years;* Ruffin, *Mahoneism Unveiled; Whig,* November 20, 1879 (being a reprint from the *Old Dominion Magazine*) ; *New Virginia.*

The son of a poor but respected merchant in one of the older counties, he had been educated at the Virginia Military Institute through the aid of friends. For a time he taught school, then he built railroads, notably the Norfolk and Petersburg of which he became president. Entering the war as colonel, he came out major-general. "Mahone's brigade" was noted for superior equipment and condition, and at Appomattox mustered out more men than any other.[5]

Mahone was perhaps the first in the South to grasp the possibilities of railway consolidation. Out of three loosely connecting and dilapidated roads, he soon created a splendid trunk line nearly crossing the state from east to west, and of this he became president with the munificent salary of $25,000. To this line he diverted from more direct routes the northward-bound cotton of the South to Norfolk, where allied steamships connected. In token of his hopes he called this road the "Atlantic, Mississippi, and Ohio."

To carry out his railroad plans public influence was necessary, and this he sought in ways characteristic of the new generation rather than of the old. Thus he strove to mould public opinion through the *Whig*[6] and perhaps other newspapers, though his control over their ownership was never announced. Always a Conservative, he had been found on each successive inauguration day "close to" the new governor. When special legislation was to be enacted, his unseen hand directed that new institution, the lobby. If a measure was to be defeated, his men were usually in the proper place, whether on legislative committees or in departmental offices. As agents in these matters, he sometimes

[5] Speech of John S. Wise in the convention of 1877 (below). J. H. Lacy in an anti-Mahone speech stated that General Lee had expressed a preference for Mahone as his successor, *Virginia Star*, August 20, 1879.

[6] Above, p. 29, and note.

obtained men already prominent in public life, but more frequently he brought forward new men, perhaps by organizing the "odds and ends" in their communities. And so a "Mahone following" was gradually built up, which was strong enough to be credited with having determined the selection of Kemper for governor.[7]

But Mahone's railroad policy had neglected or injured towns and sections, and these, especially Richmond and the Valley and part of the "Southwest," bore him distinct ill will. Competing interests dubbed him the "Railroad Ishmael."[8] Practical men saw in the financial arrangements of the A. M. & O. with the state[9] little less than a steal. Though weighty in the councils of his party and generous in its support, Mahone so conducted his relations with the Republicans and the Liberals as to suggest a lack of political principle and to create constant suspicion.[10] More than one impartial and thoughtful man despised his legislative methods and deemed his power too great.[11] There was about him, too, an imperiousness of will and manner that had helped to estrange

[7] See *Enquirer*, June 6; *Whig*, May 29, 1876; *Dispatch*, August 3, 1877. The A. M. & O. paid $155,069 for "legal fees, commissions, engraving, bonds, &c." at the time of consolidation, *Dispatch*, October 11, 1879. For Mahone's share in the campaign of 1873 (above, ch. 5) see Withers, *Autobiography*, p. 313; *Whig*, July 7, 9; August 2, 1872; *Nation*, August 14, 1873; *Dispotch*, August 3, 1877; *Enquirer*, June 6; *Whig*, May 29, 1876. Prominent in support of Kemper were Dr. Rives, Dr. Moffett, James Barbour, Joseph Mayo, all of whom favored Mahone's debt views in 1877 (below). N. B. Meade, editor of the *Whig*, became chairman of the Conservative executive committee in 1873.

[8] The phrase was William E. Cameron's. For the fight over the Richmond and Danville Railroad, to which Mahone, Scott, Garrett, and a group of Richmond men were parties, see *Whig, Dispatch, Enquirer*, April, May, December, 1874. There is virtually no mention of the A. M. & O. in the *American Railroad Journal* from 1870 to 1876.

[9] Above, p. 27, and note.

[10] The *Whig* always favored liberal party lines; so did Kemper, see *Message*, January 1, 1874; above, pp. 38, 48.

[11] *Enquirer*, July 6, 13, 1877; March 31, 1871.

each successive governor and some of his own strongest followers.[12]   An unfortunate magazine article and the farcical pretense at a duel which followed led to the charge that his military reputation was made by the press and his personal courage was questionable.[13]   Significantly enough, most of the old Bourbons and debt payers were included in some one of these groups of detractors.

It was probably with the hope of using the office to recover his road, now in the hands of a receiver,[14] that Mahone began his race for the governorship. Until July, the arguments advanced in his behalf were distinctive only in the emphasis laid upon the benefits derived by the state from his business activities. But from the first, as the Norfolk *Landmark* said, "No radical candidate was ever pursued with more remorseless severity." Had he not destroyed six millions of state assets, blocked large enterprises, and ruined his road? Where had he learned statesmanship? Was it not as "king of the lobby"? Would he pledge himself not to run independently if he failed to obtain the regular nomination? The widespread character of this attack soon showed that the case was one of "Mahone against the field," and that Mahone would lose unless he could

[12] Norfolk *Landmark*, June 17, 1877; Richmond *Times*, October 9, 1895; Governor Peirpoint does not appear to have been estranged.

[13] W. L. Royall, *Some Reminiscences*, p. 82; Withers, *Autobiography*, pp. 307 ff.

[14] Mahone's friends contended that this was the result of a conspiracy between a representative of English bondholders of the A. M. & O., Bourbons, and the Pennsylvania, C. & O., and B. & O. interests. A desire for change of management by the English holders and the good relations of Vice-President Wickham of the C. & O. with the federal and state courts and Richmond capitalists are indicated by the *American Railroad Journal*, September, December, 1875; April, June, 1876; October, November, 1877. In *New Virginia* the statement is made that Mahone was offered the presidency of the road upon certain conditions.

effect a diversion.[15]   Accordingly, early in July, there appeared in the *Whig*[16] and other friendly papers a letter which did not "re-open the debt question,"[17] but which did mark the beginning of Mahone's antagonism to the "debt paying" policy.   In this letter he declared, in brief, clear fashion, that to continue "in the present path of inaction" would mean ruin to both state and creditors; that taxes could not be increased; and that "It seems to me the part of practical wisdom, and in direct pursuit of an honorable purpose to deal fairly with the public creditors, that we should seek and insist upon, urge and if necessary demand, a complete readjustment of the debt of the commonwealth and of the annual liabilities thereunder which shall be within the certain and reasonable capacity of the people to pay."   Defining his position somewhat further, in another letter[18] he declared "diversion"[19] of the school funds not only a violation of the constitution but also bad public policy and contrary to the wishes of the people.   For free schools, he argued, were necessary for the children of soldiers and, significantly, for "the large class of persons recently admitted to the privileges of citizenship."

"The very letter for the times—clear, manly, bold . . .," wrote Colonel Fulkerson,[20] from the "Southwest"

[15] See, for example, *Whig*, March 26 (quoting Staunton *Virginian*), April 23, 21 (quoting Farmville *Mercury*); *Dispatch*, April 6, 30, May 11, June 27, July 2, 5 (quoting Gordonsville *Gazette*); Norfolk *Landmark*, June 19, 20, 1877.

[16] The letter was addressed to M. M. Martin, Charlotte, C. H.

[17] Above, *cf.* pp. 58 ff.; *Dispatch*, July 7, 11 (noting articles by Ruffin in Virginia *Patron*, and *Southern Planter*, and the talk of local candidates); *Whig*, April 17 (Hunter letter).

[18] To Major Alfred R. Courteney, of the Richmond school board, under date June 29, 1877.

[19] Above, p. 62.

[20] *Whig*, October 15, 1882.   Massey says that Fulkerson gave Mahone a copy of *Debts and Taxes* and that Mahone was converted thereby, *Autobiography*.

on the appearance of the first of these declarations. "It will elect you governor." The election of delegates had proceeded too far, however, for any such decisive result to be possible. Still, great interest was aroused. The *Enquirer,* speaking for the extreme Bourbon faction, even encouraged the suggestion that the nomination of Mahone might mean the union of the debt-paying Conservatives with the Republicans,[21] for it deemed these letters an appeal to the radical spirit manifesting itself all over the country and, because "levelled at property," an offspring of the "French principles of '93.'"[22] The *Dispatch,* more diplomatically, tried to break their force by insisting that there was nothing original in Mahone's suggestions, that the convention would, of course, decide what should be done in these matters, and that the nominee would have to abide by its decision.[23] Soon it appeared that "readjustment" had more partisans than "debt payment." All but one of the other candidates declared for it, though with vague qualifications.[24] How a readjustment could be obtained was the question. Mahone had said, "If necessary, demand"; did he mean to *compel* creditors to compromise? And if so, would not this be repudiation? This question Mahone shrewdly left unanswered.

Both the earlier and the later phases of the prelimi-

[21] See quotation from New York *Tribune,* July 29.

[22] July 25, 27, 31. The Lynchburg *Virginian* and the Lexington *Gazette* held similar views.

[23] On the morning of the publication of the debt letter, the *Dispatch* editorially favored debt action by the convention. This, it declared (July 14), was done without knowledge of the letter. It never published the letter.

[24] Only Terry flatly declared for payment of the "last dollar." For views of candidates see *Dispatch,* July 10 (Lee), 31 (Taliaferro and Holliday); *Whig,* July 13 (Terry); *Enquirer,* August 2 (Daniel).

nary campaign were reflected in the convention.[25] Fourteen hundred delegates, August weather, free liquor, and unrestrained eloquence marked the celebration by elastic spirits of a victorious party policy. Mahone, on the other hand, was prepared to fight, and there was a dangerous enthusiasm and confidence among his young floor leaders, Wise, Stringfellow, Cameron, and Riddleberger. Uniting with other "forcible" readjusters, for the debt views and the gubernatorial preferences of the delegates did not always coincide, he endeavored to have the platform adopted first. But Daniel, Holliday, and Lee marshalled their forces in joint caucus and prevented this innovation. In the balloting, Mahone at first led, his strength coming chiefly from the "Southside" but with significant additions from all parts of the state, that is, from the "solid business men" of Norfolk, the "ward-heelers of Richmond," and counties wherein the personal influence of a lieutenant was predominant. Then Daniel forged ahead, the readjuster "Southwest" swinging to him when its favorite was dropped, rather than to the former "railroad king," who had once disappointed them.[26] Thereupon Mahone in spectacular fashion threw his strength almost *en masse* to the Valley candidate, who consequently received the nomination. By this maneuver Mahone not only established "claims" upon Colonel Holliday and the Valley but also made the nomination appear colorless from the viewpoint of readjustment. Colorless, too, was the platform which urged the use of "all just and honorable means of bringing about an adjustment of the obligations of the Commonwealth which will bring the payment of interest upon the debt

[25] *Enquirer, Whig, Dispatch,* August 5, 10. Under the editorship of James Barron Hope, the *Landmark* was strongly for Mahone, understanding that Mahone was not for repudiation.

[26] In not extending the A. M. & O. to Cumberland Gap.

within the resources of the state derived from the present rate of taxation, and so do justice to all classes of our creditors.'' But it was significant that at last the Conservative party had taken a stand on the debt question.

Since the Republicans made no nomination for state offices, Colonel Holliday and his colleagues were not called upon during the ensuing campaign to interpret the Conservative platform.[27] Again, therefore, the matter was referred to the legislative districts.[28] Here confusion reigned.

Early as 1870, we find Conservatives standing for office as Independents.[29] The chief cause of this phenomenon was the temptation to bolt offered to numerous office-seekers by the eagerness of the negro minority to vote against regular Conservative nominees. One might not become a Radical and retain his social standing; but under the Conservative policy of liberal lines and a single paramount issue[30] one might occasionally bolt and yet retain the brand of ''Conservatism.'' The favorite excuse for bolting was ''ring rule'' and ''court-house

[27] In his letter of acceptance Colonel Holliday merely expressed the hope that the people would choose men for the legislature who ''have in view the memories and the resources of Virginia,'' as ''on them in chief measure will fall the work of solving this question,'' *Enquirer*, September 1. The *Enquirer* commented (September 2): ''If [the letter] means any thing it is that the writer appreciates the necessity for a canvass of the state debt question within the party.'' The readjusters, however, saw in it a pledge to leave the decision to the people expressing themselves through the legislature. *Cf.* Riddleberger in *Whig*, March 9, 1880.

[28] *Whig*, August 31, September 1; *Dispatch*, July 31.

[29] *Whig*, November 11; *Enquirer* (quoting Lynchburg *Virginian*), November 11, 1870; *Dispatch*, November 2, 3, 6, 10, 1875; Knight *v.* Johnson, Sen. *Jour.*, 1875-1876, Doc. 13; ''Personal Recollections.'' For dislike of Independents, *cf.* George F. Hoar, *Autobiography*, I, p. 313; F. Curtis, *The Republican Party*, last chapter; W. L. Fleming, *Civil War and Reconstruction in Alabama*.

[30] Above, pp. 37, 48.

cliques.'' There was much truth, beyond doubt, in the implied charge. For with the reaction against Radical rule, beginning as early as 1871, power had passed very naturally to old leaders and old families, and there the ''Confederate cult'' tended to keep it. Since this leadership, whether unduly influenced by the bondholding interests or not, was somewhat self-centered and neglectful of the wishes of the people, the Independents had pretty generally advocated whatever appeared ''popular'' or savored of ''reform.''[31]

Now in 1877, the conditions which had in the past called Independents into existence, prevailed to an unusual degree.[32] The disorganized state of the Republican party[33] rendered negro minorities unprecedentedly available. Mahone men were complaining, not without reason, of much unfair treatment in the convention primaries. The nation-wide labor agitation was affecting Virginia cities.[34] Saloon-keepers had a special grievance in the Moffett ''punch bill,'' which Mahone, appreciating their power, had taken pains to characterize as ''class legislation.''[35] The varied program of the more than six hundred granges had created business antagonisms, which, with some concealment, were transforming themselves into political factions.[36] And to the confusion caused by all this was added the doubtful meaning of the Conservative platform.[37] The cool-headed *Dispatch* admitted that ''the war brought

[31] Above, p. 65.

[32] *Landmark*, April 8, May 25; *Whig*, July 7, 13 (quoting Portsmouth *Enterprise*); *Dispatch*, July 9, 27; August 3; *Enquirer*, July 25; November 4, 6, 27.

[33] Below, p. 38.

[34] The *Whig* sympathized with this move, August 15.

[35] Letter on the debt, above.

[36] ''Personal Recollections.''

[37] On October 7, the *Enquirer* printed correspondence between Major James Dooley and Gen. Joseph R. Anderson, both of Richmond, the former

changes in the moral sensibilities of the people," and feared that "agitation only tends to increase the public indifference to public honor." On the other hand the *Whig* printed, with evident approval, the opinion of an observant correspondent that the Conservative party "is dead," because its leaders either did not know the proper limitations of the words "public faith" and "independent judiciary" or "did not choose, from whatever cause, to face the plutocracy that aspires to control, even though it ruin, the people of the state."[38]

Such conditions were necessarily reflected in the legislative campaigns. Duff Green in the Stafford-King George district, and J. L. Powell in Spottsylvania began Independent attacks on the Fredericksburg "ring." Richmond and Lynchburg had Working Men's tickets. In Henrico, Branch and Atkinson both stood as Conservatives, one for payment of the "last dollar," the other for no increase of taxes. In Albemarle, Massey was the regular nominee for the Senate, while Independents upheld his debt views against the regular nominees for the House. The *Dispatch* opposed Massey because he had once been an Independent, but supported General Starke in Brunswick because, though an Independent, he was for debt payment. In some counties, such as Pittsylvania and Augusta, the Conservatives do not appear to have made any formal nominations. An analysis of the election returns show that twenty-two Independents were elected to the House and that the idea of readjustment had won a sweeping victory.[39]

the author of the Conservative platform, the latter chairman of the committee on resolutions, which showed that neither of them understood the debt plank to endorse "forcible" readjustment, nor, indeed, anything similar to the later "Barbour bill" (below).

[38] See *Dispatch*, March 20; *Whig*, August 19, 1878.

[39] The "Southwest" was solid and the Valley nearly solid. Some of the negroes voted for Independents (who were generally for readjustment),

But whether these results rested upon some deep-seated feeling of dissatisfaction with old methods and issues, as is indicated by the setting aside of old leaders such as William Smith and John Letcher, or upon mere intrigue, as is suggested by the lightness of the vote, is not clear. Nor is it certain, on account of the vagueness of the Conservative platform and the confusion of issues in the local campaigns, just what kind of readjustment was endorsed.[40]

With the assembling of the legislature in December, 1877, the fiscal program of the readjusters became somewhat clearer. From the House finance committee came the "Barbour bill,"[41] which received the support of virtually all the Republicans and Independents and a majority of the Conservatives voting.[42] In its preamble this bill declared that "the preservation of the state government is the first necessity; the constitutional obligation to support the system of public schools, the second; and the payment of the present rate of interest

and some for General Mahone, who consistently supported the regular ticket.

[40] *Whig*, August 29, September 1, 3, November 12, 16, December 18; *Dispatch*, July 9, November 9, 11, 12, 15; *Enquirer*, November 4, 27; Virginia *Star*, October 8, November 10; *Nation*, November 1.

[41] So called from James Barbour (below) chairman of the House finance committee. This committee was appointed by the speaker, H. C. Allen, of the Valley, whom a readjuster conference had endorsed and sustained in full Conservative caucus. There were several such conferences, supposedly secret, *Dispatch* and *Whig*, December 5, 6, 10, 13, 18, 1877. The citation is from the governor's veto message, *op. cit.*

[42] House vote: aye, 20 Independents, 8 Republicans, 43 Conservatives; no, 1 Republican, 39 Conservatives. Voting affirmatively were the Conservatives Farr, Fowler, B. W. Lacy, D. A. Grimsley, Paul, Phlegar, H. C. Slemp, Hoge, Tyler; and the Independents T. L. Michie, L. E. Harvie, and P. B. Starke. Prominent in opposition were: Jos. R. Anderson, W. W. Henry, W. T. Taliaferro, Thos. S. Bocock, Marshall Hanger, John Echols, John T. Lovell, Robert Ryland, Wm. B. Taliaferro. The negative vote was strongest in the cities, Richmond and Norfolk being solidly negative, House *Jour.*, 1877-1878, p. 284; Sen. *Jour.*, p. 296.

on the amount claimed as the principle of the public debt, the third.'' Economic conditions, it continued, forbade an increase of taxes. Therefore, of each fifty cents collected through the general property tax, twenty-five must go to the support of the government, ten to the schools, and fifteen to debt interest; and the parts thus set aside for the government and the schools must be paid in money. But Governor Holliday, deeming this bill only an attempt to rob the creditors and a transfer of the ''vexed and vexing question from the legislature to the courts,'' promptly vetoed it.[43] Thereupon, with the treasury empty and the banks refusing to lend, and with the Conservative party in danger of disruption,[44] moderate men came into control, as in 1872. These moderates, however, could suggest nothing except an appeal to the creditors for a compromise, the terms of which they embodied in the ''Bocock-Fowler Act.''[45]

That the motive behind the Barbour bill was only in part fiscal is also clear. The wild talk of a ''moneyed aristocracy created by office-holders'' and the suspicion cast upon their integrity, the complaint of the seduction of readjuster legislators by the ''money rings,'' the refusal to amend the Moffett act so as to make it efficient, the suggestion of a constitutional convention to abolish the veto and revise the debt—all of these reflected the discontent of the preceding campaign.[46] Moreover, a

[43] House *Jour.*, p. 425.

[44] Below.

[45] Act of March 14, 1878; *Dispatch* and *Whig*, March 14, 15; *Whig*, March 6, 1878 (statement of auditor). The auditor was directed (*Acts*, 1877-1878, p. 237) to pay the ''diverted'' school funds in quarterly cash installments, but he interpreted this to mean, if the cash could be spared, *Report*, 1878.

[46] *Whig*, December 12, 1877; January 3, 30; February 7, 12; March 2, 15, 1878; *Dispatch*, December 6, 7, 1877. Thirty-five thousand dollars of bonds were reported to have been abstracted and funded a second time,

determination to control the Conservative party or to disrupt it was indicated when the readjusters not only admitted Independents to their conferences but compelled the full Conservative caucus to do likewise.[47] Most appropriately, the *Enquirer,* which had so consistently preached against "radicalism" and demanded the drawing of strict party lines, expired with 1877.

Immediately after the adjournment of the legislature there began a series of secret conferences among leading readjusters.[48] As a result General Mahone sent to readjuster legislators a circular letter to be signed and returned for publication over their joint signatures. This circular declared that both the veto of the Barbour bill and a recent decision of the state supreme court reaffirming the binding force of the Funding Act and in effect demanding that taxes be increased were in direct defiance of the will of the people taken in accordance with the Conservative platform of the year before, and it urged the people "to take measures to give efficiency and effect to your will, by public meetings, to be held as you may elect, and the organization of committees for each representative [Congressional] district." As "principles of faith," it advised: the sovereignty of the people of the state in matters of taxation, expenditures, and schools; reform and economy in administration; and a constitutional convention.

The immediate purpose of these activities was prob-

but this was the result of an earlier defalcation, Sen. *Jour.,* 1877-1878, Docs. 4, 6.

[47] *Op. cit.*

[48] *Dispatch,* July 5; *Whig,* July 10, 1878. Two committees acted in the matter. The first consisted of H. H. Harrison, Lewis E. Harvie, B. W. Lacy (members of the legislature), and A. Moseley, W. H. Mann, Wm. Mahone (identified with the *Whig*). These activities were suspected but not definitely known until the *Dispatch* published (July 5) the circular with the accompanying "confidential letter." The letter requested a cash contribution.

ably the election of readjuster Congressmen in the fall by
identifying the state issue with the national Greenback
movement on the ground that both were against ''money
rings'' and their allies the courts. Thus the *Whig's*
platform embraced ''forcible and irrepressible Readjustment of the state debt'' and readjustment of the national
debt by paying it in greenbacks, together with the
requirement of unanimity for setting aside a law as
unconstitutional in either state or federal courts and the
thorough purging of both from all impurities ''personal
or judicial.''[49] At first extreme debt payers and ''hard
money'' men, relying on their control of the Conservative
party machinery, were for accepting this challenge and
fighting it out on strictly party lines.[50] A calm survey
of the individual districts, however, showed clearly that
such a course would probably mean Independent or
Radical success in each.[51] On the other hand, there were
many readjusters who were unwilling to desert the
Conservative party for that of the ''Greenbackers,''
and some who thought a better fight could be made on
the state issue alone.[52] As the campaign progressed,
leading debt payers, notably the sitting members of
Congress, endorsed Greenback ideas in a more or less
qualified manner.[53] And so the movement for identifying the state issue with the national Greenback movement failed. Only two readjusters, and these of the
moderate type, were elected to Congress.

Details of the campaign, however, show how thor-

[49] May 31, March 20, April 3, 28, July 12.

[50] For example, the Richmond *State* and the Lexington *Gazette*.

[51] *Dispatch*, July 12.

[52] *Dispatch*, May 30, July 12.

[53] *Whig*, August 26 (R. L. T. Beale), 27 (Daniel); September 6 (Johnston). Only ''Ran'' Tucker was out and out for ''hard money.'' General
Johnston was a ''gold greenbacker.'' All the candidates except these two
satisfied the *Whig* on the national issue.

oughly the forces of social and political discontent were disrupting the Conservative organization. In the Richmond district, John S. Wise seemed to have a clear field. But he belonged to the local Mahone faction which had long been fighting Gen. Bradley T. Johnson as an ardent funder and "free" railroad man, and, the *Whig* insisted, a too skilful manager of party conventions. Accordingly, friends of General Johnson persuaded Gen. Joseph E. Johnston to become a candidate in the belief that Wise would not oppose his old commander. This belief proved correct. But the *Whig* in disgust supported Newman, the "Greenback" candidate, alleging as an excuse that Johnston was not acceptable to the people, as shown by the smallness of the primary vote.[54] In the Valley, John T. Harris, a moderate advocate of readjustment and greenbacks, was opposed by John Paul, a more ardent advocate, and by Gen. John Echols, who was a debt payer and "hard money" man. Echols withdrew in Harris's favor, but Paul fought it out independently. The banner district for confusion, however, was in the "Southwest." Here, debt payers said, the Mahone-Fulkerson-Blair idea was to use the local officials to supplant the existing party organization. Part of their forces, however, were diverted by Fayette McMullin who ran as a Conservative-Independent-Greenbacker and advocate of federal construction of the Cumberland Gap railroad. At the nominating convention a resolution endorsing greenbacks and readjustment was voted down, whereupon the backwoodsmen left and Col. John B. Richmond was named over two other aspirants. Colonel Richmond soon declared

[54] *Whig*, August 2, September 26; Royall, *Some Reminiscences;* "Personal Recollections" (of Mr. Royall). Wise had been associated with Edgar Allen as counsel for Platt, Republican, against John Goode, *Goode Recollections.*

himself for "honest" readjustment and greenbacks.
General Newberry as an Independent-Greenbacker, a
regular Republican, and an Independent Republican
completed the list of candidates.[55]

Soon after the elections, there was organized in Richmond a "society to preserve the credit of the state."
It was composed of thirty-nine leading citizens, among
whom were several representative ministers and two
Republican judges.   In its open address, this association proposed that similar affiliated societies, without
specified restriction as to party or race, should be
formed throughout the state, and that each should select
and support a "debt paying" candidate for the legislature the following year.   The gist of the argument
advanced was that an increase of twenty cents in taxes
(only a ten per cent increase in the total tax in many
counties) would meet all the state's needs, including a
sinking fund.   "The work proposed is grand," declared
the *Dispatch*, and the editor of the *State* was among the
associators.   But the *Whig* poured upon the "39," and
especially upon its "D. D." members, the vials of its
wrath.[56]   Outside of Richmond the move seems to have
been regarded by the Conservatives as a mistake, for
it was not only in direct opposition to the pledge of
readjustment without increase of taxes, but it also
frankly substituted a fiscal issue for old party lines and
constituted ministers, bondholders, and federal officials,
directors in a matter which people had come to consider
chiefly political.   Though the plan soon proved abortive,
it is significant as showing the loosening of old party
ties in the face of the new economic and moral issues,

[55] *Dispatch* and *Whig*, 1878, *passim*, especially August 10, 12, and early
November numbers.

[56] It persistently published (*e.g.*, December 17) the amount of coupons
used in payment of taxes by the "D. D." members.

and as affording a convenient pretext the year following for the organization of a Readjuster political party.[57]

Thus, in 1877 and 1878, a re-division of political parties along economic and perhaps social lines seemed imminent. The state was virtually bankrupt. There was much talk of "brokers" and "money rings," of "court-house cliques" and "Bourbons"; and a tendency to set aside old leaders was manifesting itself. Independents abounded, representing every phase of discontent, but always opposing the "debt payers." The Republican party was thoroughly disorganized. The overgrown Conservative party, at last forced to face the debt issue, had straddled it. An attempt at "compulsory readjustment" of the debt, thwarted by the veto of the new governor, was succeeded by a campaign for the identification of readjustment with greenbackism as movements of "the people" against the "rings" and "their allies," the courts. In all of this activity the leading spirit seemed to be William Mahone, whom (according to his friends) the rings and the Bourbons had robbed of his railroad and defeated for the governorship in 1877 through "bulldozing" and "trickery."

[57] Robert Beverly was president, A. H. Drewry, vice-president; William L. Royall, fast friend of Bradley T. Johnson and attorney for the bondholders, was secretary. Royall appears to have been the leader. The federal judges were R. W. Hughes and Alexander Rives. Among the ministers were M. D. Hoge, Joshua Peterkin, J. L. M. Curry, J. B. Jeter, and Andrew Broadus. Gen. W. C. Wickham, Republican and C. & O. official, was a member of the executive committee, *Dispatch*, November 29; *Whig*, November 30, December 5, 1878; *Dispatch* and *Whig*, January, 1879 (extracts from state press). Dr. Curry spoke on "Law and Morals" in Mozart Hall, Richmond. The rejection by the *Law Journal* of an able paper attacking the constitutionality of the Funding Act by James Lyons, of Richmond, and the attitude of the *Enquirer* (above) illustrate the feelings of debt payers at this time.

CHAPTER VII

THE "McCULLOCH ACT," AND THE STATE'S CAPACITY, 1878-1879

The compromising spirit manifested by the legislature in the spring of 1878[1] had, by the beginning of its second session, December, 1878, spread to the creditors of the state. Consequently, Governor Holliday was able to transmit, with favorable comment, two propositions, one from prominent New York bankers and brokers,[2] the other from the Council of Foreign Bondholders, of London. In striking contrast to the attitude of four years previous,[3] both pledged their efforts to secure from all creditors a readjustment of the debt on the basis of equity to all and a rate not exceeding four per cent.[4] To reconcile differences in the two propositions and to provide a practical method of giving them effect, the New York interests, acting through The Funding Association of the United States of America,[5] united with the British Council on

[1] Above, p. 79.

[2] L. G. and G. C. Ward signing for Baring Bros. & Co., August Belmont for himself and the Rothschilds, Brown Bros. & Co., Richard Irvin & Co., and Chas. M. Fry, president of the Bank of New York.

[3] Above, p. 52.

[4] Governor, *Message*, December 4, 1878.

[5] Formed about a year previous to handle such debts by Hugh McCulloch, officers of the First National Bank of New York, J. P. Morgan, and others, *Dispatch*, January 3, 1879 (quoting New York *Times*). The British organization included very distinguished names, Sen. *Jour.*, 1879-1880, Doc. 23. For McCulloch's recent residence in England and friendli-

a third proposition, which after various changes[6] (designed to give the appearance of concession, the opposition said) became the "McCulloch bill."

Under this bill the debt was divided into two classes: class I embraced consols and convertible registered bonds; class II consisted of peelers and one-half of the interest unpaid since 1871. These classes might be funded, in the proportion of at least two of the former to one of the latter,[7] into new 10-40 bonds bearing three, four, and five per cent interest for periods of ten, twenty, and thirty years respectively, with tax-receivable coupons attached, neither bonds nor coupons being taxable. The exclusive privilege of funding was given to the British Council and the New York Association above mentioned on condition that they file acceptance of the terms by May 1, 1879, and fund at least eight millions by the following January 1 and at least five millions semi-annually thereafter. With the new bonds should be issued certificates for West Virginia's third of the original debt, acceptance of which constituted a complete and final release of Virginia's obligation therefor. In and after 1885 a special two cent tax was to be levied for the sinking fund, this fund to be used "annually or oftener" for the retirement of the "ten-forties." To insure prompt interest payment the auditor was authorized (under the "Allen amendment")[8] to make

ness to the South, see Fleming, *Documentary History of Reconstruction*, I, p. 190; McCulloch, *Men and Measures*, p. 420. For McCulloch's account of the bill see New York *Tribune*, February 5, 1881.

[6] See *Acts*, 1878-1879, p. 29; Sen. *Jour., op. cit.; Whig*, February 6, 7; *Commercial and Financial Chronicle*, January 18, 25; February 15, 1879; Ruffin, *Facts*, etc.; Ruffin, *Scrap-Book*, I (L. E. Harvie in Wytheville *Dispatch*, September 4, 1879); *Fulkerson Papers* (memoranda of Colonel Fulkerson).

[7] The ratio of the outstanding consols and peelers.

[8] Incorporated as section 12 of the bill.

temporary loans and, if unable to do so, to sell, at not less than seventy-five, certificates bearing no interest but receivable for taxes.

Meantime there slumbered in a committee another bill, introduced by D. W. Henkel, a Valley readjuster, which required county and city collectors to reserve out of the taxes paid them in *cash,* subject to the order of school officials only, three-fourths of the county's or city's estimated quota of the state's appropriation to schools. The need for such protection was now very pressing, for half the schools were closing and 100,000 pupils of the year before were being kept at home.[9]   Accordingly, when the McCulloch bill had taken shape, the Henkel bill reappeared and, receiving the support of both school partisans and McCulloch bill men, passed both houses without recorded opposition.[10]

March 28, 1879, the McCulloch bill became a law.   Its passage was attended by no such scandal as that of the Funding Act.[11]   On the contrary, debate was full and

[9] State Superintendent, *Reports,* 1878, 1879. In 1877, 73 local superintendents reported a favorable change of public sentiment as to the schools, 37 no change, and none an unfavorable change; in 1878 the figures were 46, 44, and 19, respectively. For hostility to the schools see ''Civis'' in *Religious Herald,* January, February, 1878; Dr. Dabney in the *Southern Planter,* January, February, 1879; Lynchburg newspapers, spring of 1879 (a local fight).

[10] *Acts,* 1878-1879, p. 264; *Dispatch,* October 29 (W. W. Henry), October 21 (editorial); *Whig,* October 17 and 31 (Ruffner), 1879; February 13, 1885 (''New Virginia''); Ruffin, *Mahoneism Unveiled.* Henkel is thus reported in the Shenandoah *Herald,* March 5: ''With the guarantee of this house that the bill providing funds for the public schools [the Henkel bill] will be passed, it affords me pleasure to support the proposition made to the General Assembly by the creditors of the state.'' The Allen amendment (above) was a counteracting concession. Of twenty members who supported both the Barbour bill and the McCulloch bill, eighteen supported the Henkel bill.

[11] Above, p. 30.

free.[12] The vote[13] of the two houses was large, 104 to 59. Consistently, the Independents voted against it, 21 to 1. The Republicans divided evenly. Party considerations[14] and a belief that the bill contained the best attainable terms were the influences which, in varying proportions, won the Conservatives, 99 to 35.

This legislation, the McCulloch and Henkel Acts,[15] represented the triumph of that moderate move for readjustment which had manifested itself in 1871 and 1874. It discarded on the one hand the ideas of "state sovereignty," "will of the people,"[16] and antagonism to "money rings"; on the other, it recognized the actual fiscal situation and the existence of new popular necessities. If unhampered by political considerations, would it settle the debt problem?[17]

A full execution of the McCulloch Act would necessarily bring the state very great fiscal advantages: immediate relief from the pressure of accumulated interest and reduction of the interest rate by one-half, uniformity of obligations, equality of creditors, and unquestioned release from obligation for West Virginia's share; ultimately, a saving of at least $26,000,000[18] in interest. Compared with these any loss

---

[12] Contra, Whig, April 3, 4, 1879. Some debt payers, though they supported the act, boldly pointed out serious objections. For example, Senator Bradley T. Johnson declared it would necessitate an increase of taxes (Whig, October 28, 1879), and the State said the Allen amendment meant "bankruptcy."

[13] Sen. Jour., 1878-1879, p. 463; House Jour., p. 546.

[14] Below, chs. 8, 9.

[15] To these should be added the Moffett liquor law amendment (Acts, 1878-1879, p. 36) previously rejected (above, p. 79).

[16] For a proposition by Senator Paul to submit the McCulloch act to a vote of the people see Whig, February 25, 1879.

[17] The following analysis is the author's. The partisan arguments are given below, ch. 10.

[18] The Dispatch's estimate (February 3, 13, 1879) plus one-half the

of taxes on bonds or coupons, the increase in the principal by some two millions, and the annoyance arising from the tax-receivable character of coupons were negligible.

But a full execution of the act depended upon the ability and good faith of the funding monopolists on the one hand, and upon the ability of the state to meet the new interest promptly on the other.

That the first of these requisites existed seems unquestionable in view of the business standing of the promoters, the advantageous terms offered creditors, especially the non-residents,[19] and the endorsement given the scheme by the state and national administrations and the great bulk of the press. Yet it is to be remembered that the associations acted only as agents and with no penalty for non-fulfillment of contract save its cancellation, which would not affect operations already concluded by them. Readjusters at the time doubted the ability of the agents as well as their good intentions, and later asserted that the act was only a stock-jobbing device.[20] For this view, market fluctuations and the cessation of funding on an apparent prospect of full interest payment gave much warrant.[21]

The second requisite for success was much more problematic. The ability of the state to avoid defaulting

interest accrued to September 30, 1878. The new principal would be $31,227,083, the old was $29,367,958, Governor, *Message*, December 3, 1879.

[19] Owning probably two-thirds of the whole, Auditor, *Report*, 1874; William E. Royall, *History of the Virginia Debt Controversy*, p. 6. Such holders of two consols and one peeler would gain in the amount of this principal and lose little of the interest which they were accustomed to receive. Resident holders would lose somewhat, as they had used their coupons for taxes. Non-residents had sold theirs for about seventy-five.

[20] *Whig*, January 18, February 12, 24, 1879; Ruffin, *Facts*, etc.; Massey, *Autobiography*, ch. 2.

[21] Peelers were 25 in July, 41 in December, 1878, 44 in March and July, 1879. For cessation of funding see *Dispatch*, January 9, 1880.

before the funding should be completed, without resort to the endless chain of issuing certificates under the Allen amendment,[22] was exceedingly doubtful. For the act made no provision for arrearages to schools, colleges, and asylums amounting to over a million or for coupons amounting to a million and a half, as of February 1, 1879; the treasury was empty and the banks were not disposed to lend. But presuming that the crisis could have been passed, could the state pay three per cent on the new principal during the next ten years? Taking as a basis of income the revenue of 1878 and assuming that bonds held by the colleges and the literary fund would be converted, Governor Holliday estimated an annual surplus of $350,000; General Mahone,[23] of $115,000. But the reassessment of realty next year was generally expected to bring decided reduction in revenue; this loss Mahone estimated would wipe out the surplus under the governor's estimate and leave a decided deficit under his. Both the severe pruning in the governor's expense estimates[24] and the actual figures of the next year[25] indicate that Mahone was very nearly correct. Certainly the margin was narrow.

The Conservative platform of two years before had declared that there must be no increase of taxes, and the elections following had decidedly supported this

[22] In effect, these certificates would be tax-receipts discounted twenty-five per cent for cash. They were to be issued in denominations of one dollar and above, and offered for sale in each county.

[23] *Whig,* February 26, 1879. Mahone believed the state would pay three per cent on $32,000,000 provided there were no exemptions, monopoly, etc., and no future increase in the rate. Below, p. 99.

[24] *Message,* December 3, 1879. For example, the governor estimated $30,000 as the cost of the legislature annually, as compared with $100,000 from 1850 to 1860, $187,000 from 1869 to 1875, and $120,000 for 1878-1879. Also, he put ''extraordinary'' expenses at the improbably low sum of $74,000. *Cf.* above, p. 54.

[25] Below, p. 144.

view.[26]   But the foregoing analysis seems to show very clearly that under the new legislation there must be such an increase or the schools would remain stationary and the needs of the impoverished and afflicted remain unmet.   Could Virginia stand additional taxation?

Careful study of a mass of evidence indicates that the state, as a whole, had gained decidedly in both population and intrinsic value of property during the decade just ending.[27]   The debt of counties and municipalities[28] was but $13,000,000, of which $10,000,000 was owed by towns.   Though taxes had increased ten per cent, the ratio of taxation to true wealth, if the census may be trusted, was but .67 as compared with .70 and .62 for the average state and the average Southern state respectively; and the burden *per capita,* though half that of the former, was but little larger than that of the latter.[29]

It had been a great decade for the towns.   Thither, with the fall of slavery, had shifted the center of social life.   The distribution of supplies to laborers and small farmers through country merchants; the comparatively settled labor and social conditions inviting men and money from within and without; the concentrating tendency of the federal tax on tobacco manufacturing;

[26] Above, p. 78.

[27] Population increased twenty-three per cent according to the tenth census.   Reassessment of realty in 1880 showed a decrease of 43 millions, currency, which would be a small increase in gold value.   This, owing to popular depression and politics (below, p. 144), was probably too small.   The tenth census figures of 693 and 409 millions (currency) for the "true wealth" in 1870 and 1880 respectively are probably worthless. See C. D. Wright, *History and Growth of the U. S. Census,* pp. 53, 57 (note), 58, 162, 173.

[28] Tenth *Census.*

[29] Governor, *Message,* March 27, 1874; Auditor, *Report,* 1880; Tenth *Census,* VII, pp. 18, 20.   The census estimate apparently fails to include $700,000 derived from license taxes.

consolidation of railroad management and the development of shipping terminals for through traffic—all these
tended to make the town the business center also. Only
Petersburg and Fredericksburg of the old towns failed
to show gains, and many new ones had sprung into
existence.[30]

By selling off piece after piece of his estate and
mortgaging the remainder at high rates of interest, the
large farmer had been able to repair war losses and
secure improved equipment.[31]   Through such sales,
usually for a small cash payment and a promissory note,
the number of farms increased 44,668,[32] or 60 per cent,
which meant that this number of "poor whites" and
ex-slaves had become independent farmers. Gradually
the negro had settled down to something like steady
work. So production increased markedly.[33]   But only
a beginning in adaptation to the new conditions was
made.   Leaders of public thought were too busy with
race politics, and legislators with railroad wars and
state finance to provide good roads or agricultural
schools or even a respectable department of agriculture
to enable the farmer to meet the competition which rail-

[30] P. A. Bruce, in *The South in the Building of the Nation*, X, ch. 1;
Arnold, *Tobacco Industry*, ch. 2; *Ruffner Papers*. Manufacturing capital
increased from 15 to 27 millions (gold), output from 30 to 51, Tenth
Census, II, p. xii. For value of figures see Twelfth *Census*, VII, pt. 1, p.
xcvii. For influence of tobacco tax see *Dispatch*, January 15, 1879. Richmond's exports increased $300,000 from 1878 to 1879. They were chiefly
tobacco and flour, the latter for South America, *ibid.*, January 1. Norfolk
had been continually growing, chiefly through shipping and trucking,
Landmark, January, 1879. Danville and Lynchburg showed an increase
in realty values of one hundred per cent. Yet all were small towns, Richmond (the largest) having only some 30,000 inhabitants.

[31] Above, pp. 8, 25, 44. County "land books" and court records are
eloquent of the process.

[32] Twelfth *Census*, V, pt. 1, p. 699. Lots under three acres not included
in the census would probably offset the speculative investments.

[33] *Ibid.*, pp. 90, 694; Vol. VI, pp. 80, 90.

road extension made inevitable. And so profits were possible only when the general level of prices was high. But coincidently with these processes came a general drop in prices, heavy, long-continued, greater in what the farmer could sell than in what he must buy.[34] Gradually profits disappeared.[35] Laborers were underpaid. Few immigrants came to counterbalance the fearful drain, especially of young men, to the towns or to other states.[36] Land depreciated in value.[37] But the mortgage and the promissory note remained the same, the interest never failed to accrue. In some places taxes were very high,[38] and there was no money to pay them. And so the courts were busy ordering sales and the newspapers printed columns of delinquent tax payers.[39] Thus the market for land almost disappeared, and the new farmer was driven to the wall along with the old.

Now any increase in state taxation would fall pri-

[34] Averages were: 1867-1871, corn 146, wheat 145, tobacco 163; 1877-1880, 76, 105, 135, respectively, *Aldrich Report* (52 Cong., 2 sess., S. R. III, pp. 36, 104 ff.); *cf.* above, p. 59.

[35] The value of total production was eleven per cent less (gold) in 1880 than in 1870, Twelfth *Census*, V, pt. 1, p. 703. See *Whig*, January 6, February 25; *Dispatch*, February 25, June 13, 1879.

[36] Since the census figures for 1870 include West Virginia, the exact changes cannot be given. In 1880, 683,000 natives lived in other states, 62,000 born outside lived in Virginia. The tenth census (I, pt. 3, p. 479) notes the ''remarkable tendency'' toward outside cities.

[37] *Whig*, July 8; *Dispatch*, August 14, 1879; Commissioner of Agriculture, *Reports* (especially 1880); ''Personal Recollections.'' The sales books of James Roach, auctioneer of Fredericksburg, show that the most frequent price in several counties was $2.50 per acre. For areas of greater depreciation in 1875 see Map III.

[38] The *Whig* (August 8, 1879) enumerated the taxes of a man in Pittsylvania, owning property assessed at $1,000 but worth $500, as follows: state tax, $5; county and railroad debt, $6; county and district schools, $2; state poll, $1; county poll, 50 cents; total, $14.50.

[39] *Whig*, July-November, 1879, *passim;* House *Jour.*, 1878-1879, Doc. 6. The Norfolk *Landmark* had fifteen columns of local delinquents in October, the Portsmouth *Enterprise* (*Whig*, September 15), four columns.

marily on the farmer, for after ten years of experiment two-thirds of the state's revenue came directly from the counties.   Any attempt to raise the rate, therefore, would probably have led to evasion or to hardships in very many individual cases.   In either event, the debt question would have been as far from settled as ever.

As a result, therefore, of the fiscal situation and of the movements described in the preceding chapter, bondholders and leaders of the Conservative party united to frame and pass in early 1879 the McCulloch and Henkel Acts.   The Henkel Act was designed partly to protect the schools.   But while the McCulloch Act gave promise of materially lightening the fiscal burden, there was grave doubt whether its terms would be complied with by all of the creditors.   Moreover, the state could hardly have met these terms without serious injury to many individuals and continued neglect of important economic and social interests already suffering and restless.   The leading classes, however, school men included, gave the act remarkably consistent support.

CHAPTER VIII

THE "READJUSTER" CONVENTION, 1879

At the very time of the enactment of the McCulloch bill, the elements of dissent were forming a new political party for the purpose of defeating that measure.

On the assembling of the legislature in December, 1878, it appeared that the defeats already suffered and the compromising proposals of creditors had rendered some readjusters apathetic: Allen, Moffett, and Fowler, in the opinion of Colonel Fulkerson, were "morose, sore-headed, offish, ill tempered."[1] But among the rest, opinion was unanimous that public sentiment still favored the principles of the Barbour bill and ought to be organized in its behalf. So on motion of Senator John Paul, of the Valley, the drafting of a call for a state convention was tentatively authorized.[2] Then, dispersing for the holidays, the readjusters quickly obtained from local mass meetings, especially in the west, an endorsement of the convention idea.[3] Returning, in two final conferences, Col. A. Fulkerson presiding as usual, they adopted an "Address" drafted by James Barbour, chairman of the executive committee.[4] Asserting that the debt-paying association was "an organized party, openly proclaimed," and that its purpose was

[1] Memorandum of Col. A. Fulkerson, dated "January, 1879," in *Fulkerson Papers*. See above, pp. 81, 85.

[2] *Whig*, December 13, 19, 1878.

[3] *Whig*, January 3, 6, 13 (quoting Bristol *News*, Salem *Register*, Rockbridge *Register*), 16 (for action of Central Greenback Club of Marion).

[4] *Fulkerson Papers*.

to conduct a "crusade against the people" and force them to pay six per cent interest on the whole debt while starving their free schools, this address urged supporters of the principles of the Barbour bill to choose delegates "by county, district, and ward meetings as you may see fit to attend a convention of Readjusters" in Richmond, February 25, and there "take such measures as may seem to you proper to protect your imperilled rights and interests as citizens and taxpayers."[5]

About one-fourth of the legislature favored this action.[6] The "Southwest" furnished 13 of its 26; the Valley, 6 of its 20; the rest of the state, 24 out of 129. The Republicans numbered 4, the Independents, 11. Judged on this basis the group had behind it neither geographical nor political solidarity. Party ties and the possibility of compromise with creditors were too strong. But the *Whig*, assisted by a few small papers, labored earnestly in its behalf, emphasizing the social note as well as the fiscal.[7] And behind the *Whig*, but

[5] *Whig*, January 14, 17; *Dispatch*, January 17, 1879. Fowler and Moffett opposed specific reference to the Barbour bill, *Fulkerson Papers, op. cit.*

[6] Those italicized below voted against the McCulloch Act, those marked (n. v.) did not vote on it. For the convention, Senators *Bliss, Chiles, Fulkerson, Norton, Paul,* Powell (n. v.), *Slemp,* Ward, *Wood;* Delegates *Akers, Barbour, J. R. Carter, Chase, Coleman, Crank, Davidson, Dickerson, Evans, Fauntleroy,* Ficklin, *Frazier, Fulkerson,* Hamilton (n. v.), *H. H. Harrison, Harvie, W. T. James, Kelley, Lady, Lee, McCaul, McConnell, McDaniel, J. H. Smith, Spessard, A. J. Taylor, J. Walker,* Walsh, *J. R. White, Witten, Young.* Against the convention: Senator *Massey;* Delegates Adams, Bernard, Dance, *Fowler, Fry, Fulton,* Goode, *R. N. Harrison,* Henkel, Keyser, *McMullan, Moffett,* Oglesby, Popham, *Wright,* Speaker Allen, *Dispatch,* January 17; Sen. *Jour.,* p. 463; House *Jour.,* 1878-1879, p. 546.

[7] The following program illustrates the *Whig's* position at this time: abolition of the suffrage prerequisite and the whipping post; reduction of the burden of taxation, including the excise tax; bitter arraignment of the "debt-paying association," especially its "D. D." members, as

never showing his hand, was Mahone with the remnants of his railroad following, to whose fiscal views "original readjusters" were already disposed to yield.[8]

The election of delegates began forthwith and continued almost up to convention day, the *Whig* acting as a bureau of information and Samuel Goode as corresponding secretary of the executive committee. The process was necessarily irregular: informal communication among local leaders, a mass-meeting on the monthly "court-day," and the selection of desirable men from each district. Regular party officials appeared only in their private capacity. Negroes played little part. No rule as to numbers was observed. The *Whig* (promptly reducing its semi-weekly subscription rates) desired "a mighty out-pouring of the people." Resolutions reflecting at once the local situation and the editorials of the *Whig* were generally adopted. Some counties deputed members of the legislature; quite a number attempted no action.[9]

This process encountered many difficulties.[10] With few exceptions the leading newspapers were bitterly

"Pharisees"; defence of the schools against Bourbon writers and the debt-paying policy.

[8] *Cf.* below, January 5, 1878 [1879]. Fulkerson wrote: "I hope you will find time at a very early day to write out your idea as to the form of that call. If we attempt an organization, it ought to be made a success, and if successful, it will lead to an early settlement of the debt, for which the people will feel more indebted to you than to any other man in the state," *Whig*, October 15, 1882. In a letter to the Abingdon *Standard*, in *Whig*, January 13, 1879, Colonel Fulkerson expressed a willingness to pay three per cent on a recognized debt of $30,000,000 instead of six per cent on $15,000,000, which was his original idea.

[9] *Whig, Dispatch,* January, February, *passim.* Private papers, now inaccessible, would probably show a more extensive central direction and so lessen the appearance of spontaneity.

[10] *Op. cit.*

hostile,[11] and behind these papers (though as yet silent) were the regular party central organizations. Ridicule was heaped upon the move as the work of chronic bolters and agitators, intended to prevent a settlement of the debt and to advance their own interests, but likely to prove a mere "flash in the pan." The *Dispatch* maintained, with sudden and undignified changes, a veritable black list.[12] Great parade was made of former readjusters now supporting the pending fiscal legislation. These influences led in some places to apathy, in others to "trickery and bull-dozing." Many elected as delegates refused to serve. In one county, Funders[13] (led by the judge of the court, it was said) captured the mass-meeting and deputed its Funder legislators. In another, the "court-house clique" broke up the meeting. In another, negroes were chosen through the efforts of the Funder senator, the Richmond opposition proposing the plan and furnishing the necessary funds.[14]

On February 25 and 26, some one hundred and seventy-five delegates assembled in Mozart Hall, Richmond.[15] They came from three cities and fifty-nine counties, the proportion varying from west to east and according to the strength of local leaders. Politically,

[11] The *Landmark* and a few smaller papers insisted upon according the convention the respect due honest men and old allies.

[12] Later separately printed; also printed as an honor roll by the *Whig*.

[13] This name was first used for supporters of the Funding Act, but now for supporters of the McCulloch bill, and in general for the opposition to the readjuster move.

[14] *Whig*, March 1; "Personal Recollections" (William L. Royall).

[15] *Dispatch, Whig*, February 26, 27. These figures are estimates. Only a dozen counties whose legislators favored the move were unrepresented; 22 counties whose legislators were opposed sent delegates. Albermarle, home of Massey, sent 23; Petersburg, where Mahone and Cameron lived, 13; New Kent, under the influence of Major V. Vaiden and B. W. Lacy, 13; Barbour's county, Culpeper, 6; while one unaccredited delegate from Portsmouth spoke for all the populous Norfolk region, and one for the four counties of the "Northern Neck."

Conservatives of the liberal brand predominated, with a striking admixture of Republicans, Greenbackers, and Independents of every shade. Socially, there were self-made men, aristocrats, country preachers and doctors, and politicians of the usual types.[16] From Halifax and New Kent came a few negroes. It was a very loquacious body; and the more obscure members did their full share of the talking. Opinion differed on the terms of debt settlement: Mahone favored three per cent on thirty-two millions, some negroes absolute repudiation. But the dominant note was unmistakable: it was a "people's convention" assembled in response to a "wail from the people" to "crystallize the sentiments of the people and enforce them" against the "rings and court-house cliques," "brokers and the broker press." The interests of the white masses and the negroes were one; and they would brook no opposition from treacherous governor or hide-bound courts.

Without serious dissent, a vigorous "Address to the People of Virginia" presented by Senator Riddleberger was adopted. It declared that the people had always desired a definite settlement upon terms as liberal to creditors as conditions permitted. To this end they had accepted the Conservative pledge of 1877 only to find themselves thwarted by the governor. Then arose the

16 For leaders see below, ch. 9. The following were among those reported as present: Albermarle, J. A. Michie, J. H. Smith, W. H. Wood, R. G. Crank; Augusta, D. N. VanLear, Jas. H. Hamilton; Caroline, Thos. A. Welsh, S. J. R. White, Dr. Wright; Culpeper, J. W. Bell; Floyd, A. M. Dickenson; Giles, W. G. Baine; Highland, John Paul; Hanover, W. M. Newman; Henrico, William Taylor; King William, S. D. Gregory; King George, Lawrence Taliaferro; Lee, L. S. Fulkerson, H. C. Slemp; Louisa, Dr. F. F. Brook; Montgomery, E. Esbridge; New Kent, Dr. J. H. Garlick; Nottoway, G. A. Overton; Washington, D. F. Bailey, I. C. Fowler; Warren, John Paul; Wise, H. C. Slemp, Rev. Morgan Lipps; Petersburg, A. Rogers, Jr., S. Bolling; Roanoke, Dr. A. B. McConnell, Lee Willson; Stafford, Duff Green; Smith, F. M. McMullin, George W. Hubble.

"Debt-paying Association" "to take charge of the honor of Virginia, educate you up to the point of virtue from which you have back-slided," and to increase taxes so as "to pay six per cent on the whole debt." Present conditions, fiscal and economic, "certify your inability to assume a higher rate than three per cent, either now or at any future date that can be fixed by a prudent forecast." The agitation ever since the passage of "the iniquitous Funding Bill" shows that to deceive the people again, or to over-estimate their capacity "would be fatal to that repose by which every consideration should be secured." Yet, under the McCulloch bill, "the attempt is made to deprive you of all real relief by a delusive measure, which by exceptions, exemptions and discriminations takes back with one hand what it purports to yield with the other," perpetuates the most objectionable features of the Funding Act and adds others, "all cloaked, veiled and tendered under a pretense of charity." Then the Address, without suggesting any specific method of settlement, laid down as principles the following points: no liability whatever for West Virginia's share; interest on "Virginia's fair proportion" within the revenue derived from the existing rate of taxation after deducting expenses of government and charitable institutions economically administered and liberal appropriations to public schools; no tax-receivable coupons, exemption from taxation, discrimination between creditors, or funding through agencies not under the state's control; and finally, ratification by popular vote, the settlement thereafter being subject to legislative alteration. Not prominent, but very noteworthy, was the charge that the McCulloch bill "stubbornly refuses to acknowledge the necessity to our state of fitting for their exercise those whom the Federal Government invested with all the rights, privileges and immunities of citizenship.''

An elaborate plan for permanent organization, likewise presented by Senator Riddleberger, was adopted.[17] Avoiding the too obvious concentration of power under the early Conservative plan and the divided responsibility under the later,[18] this plan retained the strong features of both. For each Congressional district a chairman was to be chosen by the delegates representing it in the convention, and these chairmen (vested with considerable power in local matters) were to constitute the state committee. An executive committee of three was to be named by the president of the convention, and its chairman was to be (*ex officio*) chairman of the state committee. The plan thus outlined was duly carried out and to the important office of chairman of the executive committee, the president, Major V. Vaiden, appointed General Mahone.

The Readjuster convention of February, 1879, was called for the immediate purpose of opposing the McCulloch bill. Care was taken that both the call and the proceedings of the convention should appear spontaneous. In membership, it was representative of all classes, the great majority being Conservatives, either unknown or noted for party irregularity. The Address denounced the McCulloch bill as an attempt at deception and fraud, declared for no higher taxes, and favored public education and charities, partial repudiation, no

[17] Riddleberger was chairman of the committee on business, which handled all important matters except the permanent organization of the convention (*cf.* Bourbon plan, above, p. 20). For president, Mahone reported Major V. Vaiden, of New Kent. The temporary officers were Capt. Frank S. Blair and Capt. J. H. McCaul.

[18] Above, pp. 20, 39, 49.

exemptions or special privileges, and a popular referendum. A careful organization after the manner of
political parties was provided for, and General Mahone
was appointed chairman of the executive committee and
thus became the permanent head of the movement.

CHAPTER IX

SECTIONS AND LEADERS, 1879

Thus, under stress of economic and political conditions, the factions which had arisen among the Conservatives gradually lost their identity, until in February, 1879, the old party differences gave way before a clash between "Readjusters" and "Funders."[1] Both in the inception and in the results of the Readjuster Movement, however, one feels the weight of a force that was not altogether due to either business or politics. It may be well, therefore, to pause at this point for a rapid survey of social and political conditions as manifested in each of the "sections" into which the state had long been divided, and in the attitude and policy of the leaders whom these sections followed.

Beyond the Alleghanies lies a triangular group of counties known as the "Southwest."[2] Mountainous and possessed of a strong Scotch-Irish element,[3] this section was democratic in its habits and was drawn toward eastern Tennessee rather than toward eastern Virginia.[4] Before the war, it had never been largely given to slaveholding and in politics it had been always Democratic,

---

[1] The capitalized term "Readjuster" is here used for the organized party, its members, views, etc. The uncapitalized form, "readjuster," represents the movement in general. The same distinction is maintained between "Funder" and "funder."

[2] Ambler, *Sectionalism;* L. P. Summers, *History of Southwest Virginia;* "Personal Recollections."

[3] There is a smaller German strain.

[4] Slaves constituted sixteen per cent of the population according to the census of 1860; negroes approximately the same in 1880.

in contrast to the slave-holding and Whiggish tendencies of the Tidewater. Personal and party connections, however, together with the influence of slave-ownership upon its valley leaders and the satisfactory internal improvement policy of the state, had tied it strongly to the ''East.'' And so, though unwilling to go out of the Union, in 1861, it had declined to unite with West Virginia and had heartily supported the Southern cause. After the war, the weight of old influences again began to be felt. The large old Whig minority, disgusted at the prospect of an alliance with its former political foe, afforded the Republican party a very considerable native white nucleus.[5] The ''Southwest'' had no worn-out lands to be marketed through immigration schemes at the state's expense, and no influential moneyed centers. It had no ever present negro problem. It wanted schools and unrestricted suffrage. It wanted money to build railroads and to develop its untouched resources of minerals and timber, and it saw that this money must come from the North. Self-confident, aggressive, and suspicious, it had over and over again registered its protest in the legislature against the prevailing fiscal policy.[6] But the ''East'' was diplomatic and generous in the distribution of offices, and the ''Southwest'' remained loyal. Upon the failure of the Republican party, however, party ties had loosened and the clannish disposition of the mountain people asserted itself in personal politics.[7] Dissatisfied,

[5] In a total vote of 21,000 in the eighth Congressional district in 1869 the Republicans received 6,260. Only 4,888 negroes were registered. See Abingdon, *Virginian*, in *Whig*, March 8, 1870, for the feeling as to parties.

[6] Note its vote against the Funding Act and for its repeal, against appropriations for debt interest and for Fulkerson's anti-coupon bill; and its demand for asylums, Sen. *Jour.*, 1871-1872, p. 88; House *Jour.*, 1874, p. 451; *ibid.*, 1874-1875, p. 367; *Dispatch*, March 18, 1875.

[7] *Cf.* p. 82.

democratic, and self-assertive, this section was clearly a fit soil for the new party.

Best known among the Readjusters in this section was Col. Abram Fulkerson.[8] Of a family long prominent in Washington County affairs, he had been educated at the Virginia Military Institute and, having fought through the war, had then read law under John W. Johnston.[9] On the recommendation of Hughes, Mahone had made him one of the "incorporators" of the A. M. & O., and thenceforth they had been intimate. Entering the legislature in 1871, Fulkerson had forthwith become an opponent of the Funding Act and of the makeshift policies by which it was supported.[10] To him, as much as to Massey, was due the ceaseless agitation for readjustment and the "conversion" of Mahone; and it was he who engineered the preliminary moves in the organization of the new party.[11] He was prepossessing in personal appearance, good-natured, witty, hard-working, and, above all, shrewd and determined. Mahone called him the finest politician in the state; the *Dispatch*, a "dangerous demagogue." To the people of his section he now preached, with great effect, of hard times, the decaying schools, the lunatics in jail; and of the "proud old funders who are tickled by the Yankee bond-holders, by the phrase 'honor and credit of the state,' who don't pay any taxes, and don't care a damn who does."

Between the Alleghanies and the Blue Ridge lies the "Valley."[12] The upper part contained a notable Scotch-

---

[8] Richmond *Tobacco Plant*, May 3, 1879; *Dispatch*, July 9, 1878, October 23, 1879; Culpeper *Times*, in *Whig*, January 24, 1879; *Whig*, October 15, 1882; Summers, *History of Southwest Virginia; Fulkerson Papers.*

[9] Below.

[10] But he advocated abolition of the township system. *Cf.* p. 50.

[11] Above, p. 80; also ch. 8.

[12] Wayland, *German Element in the Shenandoah Valley;* J. A. Waddell, *Annals of Augusta County; Ruffner Papers.*

Irish element; the lower, an important German strain. Physiographically, the former looked toward the "Southwest," and the latter toward Maryland and Pennsylvania; mountain passes encouraged both to communicate with the "East." Like the "East," the Valley contained an aristocracy of landowners and officeholders, backed by an increasingly important slave system[13] but modified by intellectual traditions in the upper region and by racial characteristics in the lower. Along the mountain sides flourished a social and economic democracy like that of the "Southwest." Though opposed to secession in 1861, no part of the state had more valiantly supported the Southern arms or come out of the war with greater loss of men and property. Heretofore almost solidly Democratic,[14] it now, during Reconstruction days, became solidly Conservative; the Republicans could not poll even the full negro vote. Already, however, the upper classes had begun to leave their country homes and to settle in the little towns. Here they formed oases of intelligence and sound thinking. But their political strength was lessened. Taking advantage of this situation, the Independents grew in numbers,[15] and flourished on the vote of the negroes and the "odds and ends" of the mountain sides and the little towns. The strength of the Valley remained, however, in its middle-class farmers. No longer confronted by the slave system, these farmers were beginning to display again the "homely habits and unconquerable industry" which would "gradually restore prosperity and intelligence"[16] to the country

[13] In 1860, twenty per cent of the population was black.
[14] With the striking exception of the strongly Scotch-Irish county of Augusta.
[15] Above, p. 38.
[16] W. H. Ruffner, "Sketches of the Lyle Family," in *Washington and Lee Historical Papers*, No. 3.

districts. Though they had no negro problem, were suspicious of the eastern towns, despised the land-poor planters, and were much afraid of high taxes, they were honest, comfortable, and slow to move. Hence the vote of the Valley in the legislature had never been decided on the chief fiscal issues, and its leaders had often shown an uncertain attitude.[17] But Mahone thought that here and in the "Southwest" would begin a "ground swell" that would sweep the rest of the state.[18]

In this region Harrison Holt Riddleberger was the conspicuous Readjuster leader.[19] Having served well as a Confederate soldier and as editor of the staunchly Democratic *Tenth Legion Banner,* he had entered the House in 1871, and at thirty-two had become state Senator and elector on the Tilden ticket. So far from being an "original readjuster," he had opposed the attempted repeal of the Funding Act in 1872. But his origin, habits, and ambition threw him into opposition to the ruling groups and made him champion of the masses in his section. Thus we find him fighting the Conservative organization and the administration of the schools under Ruffner, Conservative and friend of public education though he was, apparently because he believed that both were too much in the interest of the privileged classes. This attitude soon led him to attack the fiscal policy which the state had adopted both before the war and after, and to endorse the radical doctrine that a decision of the courts against the constitutionality of a law was not binding unless it was unanimous.

[17] Governor Kemper, Congressman Harris, Speaker Allen, Senator Henkel, and to a slighter degree Col. Charles T. O'Ferrall and Governor Holliday, illustrate this tendency.

[18] *Harvie Papers.*

[19] *National Cyclopedia of American Biography; Enquirer,* March 31, 1875; *Whig,* December 3, 1874; "Personal Recollections"; *Ruffner Papers.*

Next in importance was John Paul,[20] of Rockingham, now just forty years of age. Senator Paul boasted that he had been "raised between two corn rows,"[21] and Funders were fond of pointing to his "well-known rampancy and extravagance." But he possessed, according to his closest political foe, Col. Charles T. O'Ferrall, "all the elements of popularity, strong and magnetic as a speaker, with a splendid record as a soldier and untiring energy." Both of these men had studied law,[22] and now Paul was to become Congressman and federal district judge; Riddleberger, United States Senator.

East of the Blue Ridge lie the Piedmont, Southside, and Tidewater sections.[23] Together they contained two-thirds of the state's population, of which one-half was black. They differed in soil, climate, and products; and before the war they had often differed in politics. The spread of slavery, however, together with the development of inter-communicating trade routes, had knit them firmly together under an aristocratic régime. After the war these sections remained united because their fundamental problems were the same. Of these problems, race adjustment took precedence; and the views of this region became the policy of the state. These views were

[20] *Congressional Directory,* 47 Congress; O'Ferrall, *Forty Years;* Elam, *Mahone and Virginia.*

[21] The reply said to have been made to this assertion of Paul is quite in harmony with the rough and ready discussions of the time: "A pumpkin-head, by G—d!"

[22] Paul studied law at the University of Virginia after the war.

[23] For distribution of the races see map. The "Southside" is the section south of the James. "Piedmont" is often applied to the counties along the Blue Ridge exclusively, the others being called "Midland." As the description of these sections is largely a re-survey of previous chapters, references have been deemed unnecessary. Much help has been derived from "Personal Recollections." *Cf. Nation,* September 13, 1877.

as follows: Economically, the negro must work out his own salvation, unhelped and unhindered; socially, he must remain in a rigidly separate sphere; politically, he might hold office rarely and vote to a limited extent. The rigor of this scheme, however, was modified in many a practical way, for the negro's taxes were light, his schools reasonably good, his teachers often white, and his personal freedom little restrained. His farm lay side by side with the white man's; he traded at the same store as the white man, drank at the same bar, travelled by the same railroad and steamer. When he was accused of crime, white lawyers defended him. His own church and public "hall" rose in every neighborhood, always with white assistance. Grievances the negro undoubtedly had. Punishment by whipping and chains he deemed "class legislation" and "degrading"; and he resented the fact that his insane were thrust into the jails and that jury-service, which he deemed a privilege, was denied him. But for all this, he was fairly content with his position as a whole; only the practical loss of political privileges rankled.

Not less important was the social situation among the whites of the "East." Many of the old plantation class, realizing that the prestige of the plantation was gone, had quickly moved to the near-by towns, making these, as in the Valley, the new intellectual centers. Under the exigencies of reconstruction politics, political leadership, too, passed from the counties and the old leaders gave place to a compromising and practical body of men residing chiefly in the towns—men with strong Northern connections, intent upon the material development of the state, and caring little for "dead issues." Then came the Confederate reaction, bringing prominence and power to "war heroes." While adhering to the views of the old leaders these men deemed themselves practical, and soon formed alliances with the "interests," by conceding to the latter the shaping of economic and fiscal policies though reserving the offices for themselves. Thus "honor" and the "credit of the state" were combined in a new party watchword. Meantime a stronger middle class was forming. To the numerous small farmers were added new landowners, saloon-keepers, small manufacturers, truckers, oyster-planters, cattle-dealers, merchants, self-made lawyers, and not a few solid adventurers from the North. The towns felt their presence: even in Richmond political recognition was accorded the German and Irish elements, and a "bone and sinew" candidate now and again opposed a "Franklin Street man." Still more important were the men of this class in the counties from which the old leaders were departing. Here they rose to prominence in the churches and the numerous fraternal and benevolent associations, shared local political leadership, and even broke into the family circles of the weakened upper classes. As yet, however, their opportunities were greatly restricted; for energy, initiative, and equipment were valued but lightly in comparison with "experience," and in public life offices were deemed "honors." Finally, turning to the lowest classes, we find conditions very bad and very slow to improve. Never had illiteracy been so great or knowledge of public affairs so slight.[24] Obsessed by race prejudice, the lower classes followed party leaders almost as blindly as did the negroes. The abolition of slavery, together with the breaking up of the plantations and the establishment of public schools, unquestionably meant their ultimate emancipation, but only after they had learned to labor intelligently and to save. Meanwhile hard times and competition with

[24] The "pauper" system of schools (ch. II) was discontinued during the war and was never revived.

the freedmen kept them literally bowed to the ground. The more serious minded found solace in the churches, where a Puritan-like religion was preached; others, in the saloons, where drunkenness and brawls were frequent. In the public schools, indeed, they dimly recognized their children's chance for better things. But it was difficult both to pay taxes and to spare the child's labor and the money for his books and clothes. Besides, in some places the schools were closing. Could these masses be aroused so that they would throw off the leadership of the aristocrats and the towns? Before 1877 efforts to this end had been rarely successful and only when disguised by some minor issue. Now, in 1879, Mahone was hopeful, but not sanguine, that the masses might be stirred to a livelier interest in the affairs of the government.

The list of leading Readjusters in the "East" was short but significant. Foremost in the ridge counties was the plebeian farmer and parson, John E. Massey; in the Midland, James Barbour led. Of a family long prominent in the affairs of state and nation, Barbour had battled independently and fearlessly for a more representative party management and against the fiscal policy embodied in the Funding Act.[25] In Richmond, the *Whig* fought almost alone; for the course of John S. Wise was as yet unannounced. In the "Southside," where the densest negro population lay, the self-made Mahone found a powerful ally in his aristocratic fellow townsman, William E. Cameron. An editorial writer of uncommon power, Cameron was also a successful politician, and was now serving his third term as mayor of Petersburg despite its large negro majority. He and John S. Wise, both young, eager, and brilliant, with perhaps a touch of unsteadiness, were destined to be

[25] Barbour had been anti-Mahone in the railroad war.

viewed in the North as excellent examples of the anti-Bourbon forces in the movement. From Williamsburg, Dr. Richard Wise, of the well-known Virginia family of that name, co-operated with V. D. Groner,[26] the self-made manager of a great Norfolk steamship line, himself no believer in Readjustment but a friend of Mahone.[27]

While the leading Readjusters of the "East" were thus evenly divided as regards the class from which they sprang, the three most conspicuous and powerful of them were, and claimed to be, "men of the people." William E. Massey[28] called himself "the father of the Readjuster movement." The son of a small farmer and mechanic of Spottsylvania County, he had managed to secure a good education, and having drifted about in Piedmont and the Valley, as teacher, lawyer, and itinerant and regular preacher in turn, he had finally settled as a farmer in Albemarle. Forced repudiation of Confederate bonds (some of which he owned), increased taxes for interest on the compounded state debt, the high private interest rate, and the general suspicion of one who lives remote from the center of things combined to convince him that the interests of the "people" were not being represented at Richmond. Therefore, though sharing the traditional Virginia opposition to a minister's participating in politics, he felt that the situation imposed upon him a moral duty. And so, in 1873, he entered the House to undo the Funding Act. Here, impressed by the indolent and slipshod methods of handling the state's securities, he hit upon the plan of killing the act by creating difficulties in the use of coupons, on the ostensible ground of preventing fraud.

[26] See *Dispatch,* November 15, 1879, June 2, 1881; *State,* 1881.

[27] *Whig,* June 3, 1881.

[28] Massey, *Autobiography;* Contemporary press; "Personal Recollections"; above, p. 63.

The morality of this appeared perfect, for he was an "original readjuster." From the genial simplicity of his looks and the apparent harmlessness of his efforts, the capital city reporters soon dubbed him "Parson." But when, in 1877, the state treasury became empty and the lawyer-farmer urged in a vigorous pamphlet that the affairs of the state be settled as would those of a private bankrupt, men began to say that he would be a strong independent candidate for governor. Save for his fiscal views, however, Massey was a genuine Conservative; only with considerable reluctance did he enter the convention of 1879. But once committed, he acted with remarkable energy. Wandering about the state, he drew large crowds, especially among the farmers. Thoroughly understanding the shallower aspects of finance and the deep feelings of the people, with a marvellous memory for figures and a lack of scruple in using them, full of homely anecdotes and Biblical quotations, occasionally caustic, always imperturbable, he had no peer as a stump-speaker in his own party and rarely met his match among his opponents.

Through its long opposition to policies approved by the leading classes, the Richmond *Whig* had become by 1877 theoretically a democratic paper. In the shaping of this attitude well-born men had played a leading part— Mosely and Meade as editors, Cameron, Ruffin, and Ruffner as contributors. None the less the belief gained ground that for certain purposes at least the *Whig* was but the "personal organ" of General Mahone; and as Mahone and democracy were both unpopular in Richmond, it had ceased to be read in the "best homes" there. Its editor now was W. C. Elam, a plain man of North Carolina and as good a school man "as ever put pen to paper."[29] With Elam the social note was ever promi-

[29] W. H. Ruffner to Elam, *Ruffner Papers.*

nent—"the Brokers and the Broker press," the "Scribe and Pharisee" parsons, the office-holding set who "generally train with the court-house clique and always believe that money and position are stronger than the people." In lucid explanation of figures, often combined with unwarranted distortion of them, in effective reiteration of a leading idea in striking language, and in arousing suspicion of his adversaries' motives through insinuation, virulent personal attacks, and often deliberate misrepresentation, he was unexcelled. And for all such utterances of the *Whig*, though a recluse by habit and physically unfit, he held himself strictly accountable, according to the honor code of the "Bourbons" whom he so much affected to despise.[30]

Quite different from the rest was Gen. William Mahone.[31] In him a varied career as soldier, railroad president, and political wire-puller had developed remarkable capacity for intrigue, organization, and command; and an extraordinary energy rendered these powers always available. Possessed of a peculiar personal appearance, a high-pitched voice, and many idiosyncrasies of manner, he presented to the observer few of the characteristics of an orator or party leader. Though he quickly learned the language of the reformer and spoke easily of "the cause" which he came later to interpret as the "regeneration of Virginia," he lacked magnetism and was never genuinely popular with the rank and file. Lieutenants, however, he won easily, especially among young men, and these he inspired with

---

[30] See *Dispatch*, June 24, July 3; *Whig*, February 9, 1880. The Northern Neck *News*, June 11, 1880, has an account of his duel with Col. Thomas Smith, of Fauquier, caused by an editorial assertion (June 1, 1880) that on the collapse of the Confederacy, "the President, Governor, and whole bomb-proof corps grabbed the remaining swag and sneaked away." It is said that Elam after the duel denied the authorship of this.

[31] Above, p. 68.

confidence and aggressiveness. In the campaign of 1879, we hear little of headquarters of committeemen. Mahone was everywhere—planning, speaking, bargaining. It was a new type of leadership, and one with which Funders for four years were utterly unable to cope.

The Funders accorded to none of their number such precedence as was enjoyed among Readjusters by the leaders just described. Of most distinguished *antebellum* services was R. M. T. Hunter, state treasurer, who had been opposed to the tax-receivable coupons and had favored a readjustment of the debt in the interest of "peelers," but now deprecated party divisions because, he thought, "the political warfare upon the South has not yet ceased."[32] Although a Confederate of distinguished Virginia family and educated in the school of Calhoun and McDuffie, John W. Johnston had accepted federal appointment as judge in 1869, and from this position had been advanced to the federal Senate by the compromising legislature of 1869-1870. Conducting himself with quiet dignity, however, he managed to escape serious suspicion as to his party integrity, and having become rooted in the regard of the business men of the "East" and of the entire western section, he was now serving his third term.[33] The family and business connections of Robert E. Withers, together with a certain personal charm, political aggressiveness, and the glamour of military service, had caused him to be elected over Hunter in 1874, as the colleague of Johnston.[34] An intense interest in public education led Dr. William H. Ruffner, of Lexington, at first to favor readjustment; but

[32] Letter in *Dispatch,* October 4, 1879.

[33] He was elected twice by the legislature chosen in 1869, see above, p. 22. The third time John W. Daniel was his chief opponent.

[34] Withers, *Autobiography,* p. 317.

upon the passage of the Henkel Act, he began to throw the weight of his strong personality and the prestige of his office into the Funder scale.[35] All of the Congressmen supported the Funders. Of these, John Randolph Tucker, of Lexington,[36] was probably the ablest and had the clearest record for sound fiscal views; John Goode, of Norfolk, was deemed the most eloquent and popular. The *Whig* hated Tucker most bitterly for his opinions, and despised Goode for having broken from his old alliance with Mahone.[37] A war hero, young, eloquent, popular, and with a personal defeat chargeable to Mahone,[38] John W. Daniel, of Lynchburg, was most active in stumping the state, and successful beyond all others in uncovering Readjuster plans. An asset of great moral worth was the eloquent preacher and future ambassador to Madrid, J. L. M. Curry, professor in Richmond College.[39] Gen. T. M. Logan, now a railroad promoter of Richmond, and Senator John T. Lovell, editor of the Warren *Sentinel,* shared the committee leadership; J. Bell Bigger, formerly of Lynchburg, was secretary. Among the newspapers may be mentioned the Richmond *State,* which inherited the Bourbon clientage of the *Enquirer,* the Norfolk *Landmark,* which had but recently broken with Mahone and still insisted upon a discriminating liberalism, and the Richmond *Dispatch,* now nearing the height of its power as party organ *par excellence.* To these should be added the Baptist *Religious Herald* and the Methodist *Christian Advocate,* whose occasional entrance into campaign controversy, contrary to their usual custom, serves to

[35] *Whig,* January 31; *Dispatch,* October 17, 21, 1879.
[36] Above, p. 81. Mr. Tucker founded the law department of Washington College just after the Civil War and lectured there for years.
[37] "New Virginia."
[38] Above, p. 74.
[39] Alderman and Gordon, *J. L. M. Curry,* p. 246.

show how dangerous to moral and social order leaders of the upper middle class deemed the new movement. In Gen. W. C. Wickham, of Hanover and Richmond, the Funders had a Republican ally of much influence in his party and of unquestioned business and social standing.[40]

This brief survey of the geographical sections of Virginia at this time shows that the "West," especially the "Southwest," being democratic and unencumbered with a negro problem, was ready to follow the Readjusters, and that in the "East" where the negro though of great importance was an uncertain factor, their chief hope lay in winning ambitious young men or self-made men of the middle class, who were barred from political advancement by the prevailing preference for "experienced" men or war heroes, and who might be counted on to arouse the lower classes of whites. It shows also that though the leaders of the new party were about equally divided between the well-born and the self-made, the two most conspicuous Readjusters were both "men of the people."

[40] Wickham won the rank of brigadier-general in the Confederate army. As a member of the Confederate Congress he advocated a cessation of hostilities in 1864-1865. Because of the friendship of Grant he was useful in the movement of 1869. He was successively president, vice-president, and second vice-president of the C. & O. Railway. See memorial, "A type of the Southern Civilization," by Thomas Nelson Page.

CHAPTER X

THE READJUSTER CAMPAIGN, 1879

The contest for control of the legislature of 1879-1880 began with the Readjuster Convention.[1] To prevent the enactment of the McCulloch bill,[2] Readjusters of the legislature had already begun to filibuster. But, supported by the bulk of the press and some expressions from the public mass-meetings, Governor Holliday called an extra session. The Conservative state committee met quietly on the night after the call and endorsed the bill.[3] Then the debt-paying association became dormant. Black-lists of the opposition began to appear. And after some three weeks the Funders had secured the great advantage of *une fait accompli*.[4]

Interest centered next on the spring elections for local offices. Control of these through "rings," Readjusters said, formed the very basis of "Bourbon" and "Broker" power. Accordingly, candidates sprang up "as plentiful as the locusts of Egypt." In some places ability to write was the only requisite required. "Handshaking" on county court-days was widely complained of. Incumbents usually won; for in many eastern counties the possibility of Republican success kept the organ-

1 Ch. 9.

2 Above, p. 85.

3 Below.

4 *Dispatch*, March 5, 6. W. E. Royall took the stump for the Funders and in 1880 established the *Commonwealth* in their interests; Bradley T. Johnson returned to Maryland; C. U. Williams became financial agent for the funding syndicate. *Cf*. p. 81.

izations intact, and in others party regularity was still
esteemed. But the increased number of the disappointed, the acceptance of Readjustment by many of
them, and the bitterness of feeling developed—these
were all favorable to the new move.[5]

Local organization in the interest of the Readjusters
had begun during the convention days when some county
chairmen were appointed by the Congressional district
committees.[6] Early mass-meetings especially in the
democratic ''West,'' had enthusiastically assumed to
endorse, revise, or supplement these appointments, the
standard being usually good community standing.
But soon a dearth of material was met, and mass-
meetings and committees ceased to be reported. Save
for the peripatetic Massey, Readjuster speakers also
became quiet. Encouraged by this and by the apparently successful operation of the McCulloch act, the
Funders exultantly asserted that the move was ''dead.''
On July 4, however, the *Whig* briefly stated that
the organizing was going on ''with vigor.'' This
was true. Through his power as party chairman,
Mahone had been quietly selecting his men, and late in
July the Funders, to their surprise, faced a compact and
widely extended organization.[7] For these later selections, the qualifications were generally shrewdness and
availability.

The Funders, meantime, were planning to use the
name and organization of the Conservative party. But

[5] *Cf.* above, p. 76. *Dispatch, Whig* (news and editorial columns),
April, May, especially election returns (May 24 ff.); *Virginia Star,* August
23; Northern Neck *News,* June 13.

[6] Above, p. 101. The county (or town) chairman named three associates
from each magisterial district, these smaller groups constituted precinct
or ward committees.

[7] *Whig,* February 27 (list of county chairmen); March 22, 24; April 24;
May 20. The difficulty was admitted by Readjusters, *Whig,* July 23,
October 30 (New York *Herald* interview with Elam).

the Conservative state committee hesitated to take vigorous action. A half-hearted attempt at checking the move early in March had met only derision.[8] The Readjusters, clinging to their place in the old organization,[9] refused to admit that they had left the party;[10] they asserted that the committee held by usurpation and represented rejected principles,[11] and they challenged it to call a state convention.[12] It was, indeed, no slight matter to "read men out of the party"; and the final decision was taken in the face of the vigorous protest of two members and by one less than a majority of the whole committee. On August 6, by a vote of 13 to 2, the McCulloch Act was declared "a great public measure devised and accomplished by the will and judgment of the Conservative party," and support of it was made the test to be applied in local organization and nominations.[13]

Public discussion formed a striking[14] and important feature of the campaign. In March, prominent Readjusters began to invade the precincts of Funder legisla-

[8] By the vote of nine members the Readjusters were declared a "party" and local reorganization in the interests of the McCulloch bill was urged. The *Whig*, March 6 ff., dubbed this "Lord Lovell's lament" from John T. Lovell, over whose signature as chairman the address was published. For unsuccessful attempts at local reorganization see *Whig*, March 22, 24, 26 (quoting Fredericksburg *Recorder* and *Southern Intelligencer*).

[9] For disorganization in consequence, see *Dispatch*, October 23; *Virginia Star*, October 25.

[10] *Cf.* Bourbons in 1869 and debt payers in 1877, above, pp. 21, 36, 73.

[11] "If Readjusters have gone out of the party, where in the devil did the Funders go when they formed an association with Wickham, Rives, and Hughes . . . ?" Abingdon, *Virginian*, in *Whig*, March 11. *Cf.* above, p. 83.

[12] *E.g.*, *Whig*, March 11.

[13] *Dispatch*, *Whig*, August 7. John L. Marye drew the report. Groner and Wise (above) protested. For two later addresses, see *Dispatch*, August 9, 20. Some Funders regretted this action, notably the *Landmark* and the Petersburg *Index-Appeal*.

[14] *Cf.* above, pp. 41, 49.

tors, compelling them to defend themselves and sometimes to call in their more eloquent friends. This attack
lasted through May. In August, the Funders "took
the stump" in force. Debate then became general and
continued until November. The Readjusters used their
half dozen strong speakers to great advantage. Beginning in the "Southwest," in the Valley, and in the ridge
counties of Piedmont, where discontent was unrestrained
by the negro problem, they advanced gradually east-
ward, singly, by twos, threes, or even fours, as occasion
demanded, through the discontented tobacco counties
into Tidewater and thence back into the fairly prosperous counties along the upper Potomac, often suddenly
returning to some strategic point threatened by the
Funders' more numerous artillery. Although new party
organs were established and the circulation of the old
ones increased, these discussions, often joint and lasting
from four to six hours, largely took the place of campaign literature.[15]

At first the Funders assumed a haughty attitude, and
relied too much on appeals to sentiment. But the Readjusters asked questions, read figures, and took the offen-
sive; and soon detailed and serious discussions became
common. These discussions centered upon three points:
the validity of the debt, the McCulloch "settlement,"
and the purposes of Readjuster party.[16]

[15] For convenient list of newspapers, see *Dispatch*, August 21; *Whig*,
January 4, August 5. Ten thousand copies of General Mahone's convention
speech were ordered printed. The address of the Readjuster members of
the legislature could be had for five dollars per 1000, net. Funders printed
the Petersburg address of J. W. Johnston. Examples of new papers are
the Giles *True Issue* (Readjuster), and the Northern Neck *News* (Funder).

[16] Among the best reported speeches are those of J. W. Johnston in
Norfolk and Petersburg (*Dispatch*, October 2, 11); Ran Tucker in the
"Southwest" (Abingdon *Standard*, October 16); Mahone in Richmond
(*Whig*, February 25); Blair at Wytheville (*Whig*, May 20); and Massey
as collected in his *Autobiography*. See also Conservative committee ad-

The Funders would begin by showing how the debt was originally contracted honorably and for public utilities which still served their purpose.[17] Admitting this, the Readjusters told of how interest had accumulated during war and reconstruction, and of how this had been assumed as an obligation and compounded, under the Funding Act, contrary to every principle of law and equity.[18] But, said the Funders, we are bound for the debt as it stands (less West Virginia's share): legally, even to the extent of our private property, because of our contract; morally, because we are forbidden to steal—the state's honor is that of the individual; commercially, because Wall Street opinion "controls the influx of capital."[19] No state, replied the Readjusters, has ever been compelled to pay against its will. Other states have repudiated without loss of credit or blame from Funders.[20] Are not many of you *private* bankrupts? Is it not rather cowardly to cater to the opinion of those who "having stripped us, think it rascally that we should not submit to be skinned"?[21] "Honor won't buy a breakfast."[22]

dresses (above). Important Funder campaigners not mentioned above were: A. A. Phlegar, called by the Readjusters the "brains of his party in the Southwest"; W. W. Walker, minister and lawyer; C. W. Stringfellow; W. E. Royall (above); Gen. J. A. Walker, commander of the Stonewall Brigade; J. H. Tyler, C. H. O'Ferrall, and P. H. McKinney, later governors; ex-Speaker Allen; Attorney-General J. G. Field, elected as a Readjuster; R. A. Coghill; A. M. Keiley, mayor of Richmond.

17 This argument was used in the "West" especially, *Dispatch*, July 29 (editorial), August 13 (letters); *Whig*, September 6 (editorial).

18 While Readjuster opinion continued to differ on the amount the state was not properly bound for, this was always excluded. *Cf.* above, p. 62. Funders urged that emancipation was not an absolute loss to the state, *Whig*, September 5 (W. W. Walker); *Dispatch*, October 2 (J. W. Johnston).

19 Norfolk *Landmark*, in *Dispatch*, October 17.

20 *Whig*, October 23, November 3.

21 *Whig*, February 28.

22 This phrase, first used by Blair, was much distorted in its applications by the Funders.

The McCulloch Act, asserted the Funders, will settle the question. It gives to creditors even less than does the Barbour bill. Its acceptance by them is clear from the amounts already funded. It brings the debt within the capacity of the state. Even Mahone has admitted,[23] and the auditor's figures clearly demonstrate,[24] that three per cent interest can be paid now without increase of taxes, and before the higher rate begins conditions will so improve that the ten-forties can be replaced by three per cent bonds. Under the Henkel Act, they continued, the schools will receive more than the Barbour bill allowed them; therefore, the leading school officials advocate the new settlement.[25] Through exemptions and special privileges, replied the Readjusters, the ten-forties are equivalent to six per cent bonds. Moreover, the creditors of the state, under this act, would receive only fourteen of the thirty-two millions that the state would have to pay; brokers would get the rest.[26] Comparison cannot be made with the Barbour bill as that was but the first part of the program of 1877-1878.[27] The Funders' estimates are deceptive as usual, the fraud now consisting in making a division between "ordinary" and "extraordinary" expenses and excluding in the process whatever is inconvenient. Actually, there would probably be a deficit of $600,000 yearly for the first ten years under the proposed "settlement."[28] Did not Johnston

[23] Above, p. 99.

[24] Address of Conservative state committee, above, p. 120.

[25] *Landmark,* July 9 (speech of Supt. William F. Fox, president of the Educational Association of Virginia).

[26] See the Godwin-Royall debate at Surry Court House, *Dispatch,* August 28; *Whig,* September 1, October 3.

[27] *Whig,* October 3.

[28] The chief trick in the juggling by which this was obtained lay in confusing the special embarrassments of the funding period (above, p. 90) with permanent conditions. The confusion was very thoroughgoing. See Massey, *Autobiography,* ch. XIV; *Whig,* August 11.

and Phlegar originally admit this? And is not McCulloch reported to have already "given the order" for an issue of certificates under the "Allen amendment" which will cost the state five and a half per cent a month[29] and paralyze the schools? Just wherein lies the justification for believing that ten years will enable us to pay a state tax of ninety cents?[30] Shall the state be thus "bound for forty years"? Shall the people never know anything but debts and taxes and unsatisfied wants?

Questioned as to their political intentions, the Readjusters asserted that this was not a "party fight"; men would next year vote their old tickets.[31] Here, however, they were on the defensive. The Funders were, indeed, forced by campaign exigencies to modify their early emphasis upon the heinousness of "deserting" the Conservative party for an alliance with the Republicans.[32] None the less, they thoroughly ventilated the "records" of the new party leaders.[33] "Look at them all. From leader to corporal, what has any one of them ever done? Absolutely nothing." Massey was a "political parson"; Paul, a "ranter"; Fayette McMullin, "an ignorant, uneducated old man"[34]—all were "disappointed politicians" seeking to "get possession of the state, rob her, and blacken her fair name."[35] And Mahone! had he not virtually robbed the state of assets equivalent to ten millions of state bonds?[36] Did he not, during the last legislature, father a scheme for using the sinking fund

---

[29] *Ibid.*, September 17. Certificates could be sold at seventy-five and redeemed six months later at par.

[30] Report, in *Dispatch*, September 2, of Mahone's Charlottesville speech.

[31] For example, *Whig*, September 10; Blair at Wytheville, Wytheville *Dispatch*, in *Whig*, May 20.

[32] See *Dispatch*, August 28, for a recent local use of this.

[33] *Dispatch*, July 10 (editorial).

[34] *Dispatch*, July 23.

[35] *Dispatch*, July 19; August 8 (quoting Hillsville *Virginian*).

[36] Royall in *Dispatch*, October 11, and Abingdon *Standard*, October 16.

to purchase a railroad and make himself president?[37]
Now compare with these our leaders, they said, both
Senators, all the Congressmen, four ex-governors, the
leading clergymen, nearly all the newspapers at home
and abroad![38] And what will the Readjusters do if they
win? Pack the state courts[39] and attempt to repudiate?
Then we shall have among us federal tax gatherers,
backed by federal troops.[40] The day, replied the Readjusters, when great names carried weight is past.[41] As
for the press, ''McCulloch's Republican organs in New
York and his Conservative organs in Virginia play the
same tune. . . . *in hoc signo vinces*—$ is borne on all
the banners of the many against the few.''[42] Office-seek-
ing! How dare the Funders reproach us for this? Has
not Daniel run for ''every office in sight,'' and at last
had a town created that it might bear his name and elect
him mayor?[43] The debt can be readjusted, without any
packing of the courts, by using pressure such as the
Funders are now using upon consol holders.[44]

From their dull talk of sickness and hard times the
people turned to these discussions as to an intellectual
treat, plodding miles, and standing hours in the summer's heat. But they were largely a crude, unread
people, untaught by reconstruction politics to differ
philosophically. Coarse jokes, rude interruptions, sting-
ing personal attacks were relished. Feelings usually ran
high. Among the spectators fights were not infrequent.

[37] *Dispatch,* September 5 (editorial on authority of Daniel).

[38] *Dispatch,* July 28.

[39] *Cf.* above, p. 46.

[40] Argument used by Royall and Goode and endorsed by the *Dispatch.*

[41] *Whig,* September 10 (on candidacy of W. W. Henry); *Virginia Star,*
October 11.

[42] *Whig,* February 28.

[43] Massey, *Autobiography,* ch. XIV.

[44] Elam, New York *Herald,* in *Whig,* October 30.

Often a general "row" seemed imminent. Back to the crossroads store went a vague impression that we did or didn't owe a debt, and a vivid recollection of how some speaker "eat up" his opponent.[45]

Nominations for the one hundred and forty seats[46] in the legislature began early in August. In the "West," Readjusters and Funders conducted themselves like well-established parties of nearly equal quality.[47] In the "East," however, chaos reigned. The Funders had much trouble. Their "Conservative" meetings were often attended by Readjusters—sometimes in good faith, often to force an adjournment or even to dictate the nomination. Many refused to enter the "modern scramble for office." Sometimes faction and the strength of the debt feeling compelled them to postpone nominations, set aside old favorites, and honor converted Readjusters.[48] But, on the whole, their selections were decidedly representative of the successful upper classes. In Readjuster conventions, on the other hand, one could note an unusual proportion of new men and ruined representatives of old ruling families, and many Independents and Republicans. Here some excellent nominations

[45] "Personal Recollections"; *Dispatch*, August 28 (Surry); *Virginia Star*, November 1; *Whig*, June 12 (Grayson *Clipper*); October 18 (Rockingham). At least two were shot in quarrels. For duelling later, see above, p. 114.

[46] The full number of both houses under constitutional amendment of 1876, *Thorpe*, VII, 3902.

[47] The Funders were somewhat superior socially and in past political honors especially in the Valley. In six counties of the "Southwest" and one of the Valley there were Independents.

[48] *Whig*, October 1 (Grayson); *Dispatch*, October 8 (King William); *Whig*, March 22, 24, 26, April 19, and Virginia *Star*, August 13 (Stafford); *Whig*, September 6, and *Dispatch*, September 15 (Patrick-Henry); Virginia *Star*, August 23, October 1 (Fredericksburg-Spottsylvania); *Dispatch*, October 6 (Prince George-Surry).

were made[49] and some exceedingly bad ones.[50]   The
latter were due in part to the dearth of suitable material and in part to the attempt to win the colored vote.

Influenced by the opposition of President Hayes to
repudiation in any form, the Republican state leaders
early expressed their personal approval of the McCulloch Act. On the other hand, they hoped that the negro
would be kept out of the campaign, lest, perhaps, he
learn to follow other leaders.[51] With this the Funders
were, of course, content.[52] The negroes, however, as far
as they had any opinion on the subject, were opposed to
paying the debt. It had been created by their old
masters, it interfered with schools and asylums, and it
necessitated a tax on whiskey. Moreover, it was generally supported by their political opponents and opposed
by the local Independent and Republican leaders whom
they were wont to follow. Still, fear of estranging the
whites and, in many cases, the habit of years impelled
the Readjusters to seek this vote very cautiously. True,
the negroes who had come to their convention had been
received courteously, and had been accorded in the
address a vague recognition of their desires as to
schools, suffrage, and taxes. But, taunted with these
facts, the Readjusters half apologized; saying that to
break the color line had been originally one of the aims
of the Conservative party; that the debt question must
be settled by votes, and they preferred the "honest

[49] E.g., the "Gallant" Col. Bob Mayo, of Westmoreland, and J. T.
Stovall, formerly Conservative chairman in Patrick-Henry.

[50] This analysis is based on a detailed study of two Tidewater and two
Piedmont counties and the returns for the House (*Dispatch*, November 16),
supplemented by a mass of press notes.

[51] *Cf.* above, pp. 50, 83. *Whig*, March 3 (views of President Hayes),
July 12, 30 (quoting Rockbridge *Enterprise*); August 20 (*Southern Intelligencer*); below, p. 135 (purported Mahone-Cameron arrangement).

[52] *Whig*, March 22; *Dispatch*, August 9, November 15 (quoting).

negro" to "Bourbon Republicans"; that the Funders had counted upon "bagging them all" through their association with "Rives and Co."; and that it was due to Bourbon trickery and broker money that negro delegates had come to their convention at all.[53] Accordingly, confused by divided leadership and little sought by either side, the negroes were generally apathetic.[54] But with September the situation changed sharply. Beginning, apparently, with an insinuating speech of Massey's in Petersburg, the Readjusters spread rumors that they would grant the colored men more "rights" and that the Funders meant to increase the poll tax to three dollars and "bind" them for forty years. Churches and societies were called in to spread and enforce these rumors.[55] Republicans, some of them negroes, were supported for the legislature in at least twelve counties and one town. The Funders at once countered by appeals to the negro pride in their "best men" and by confusing local situations. They spoke from the same platform with hired negro speakers, established clubs, ran Republican candidates to split the vote of the Readjusters, and in at least six counties voted themselves for Republicans, two of whom were negroes. Moreover, private citizens pledged themselves to pay any increase in the poll tax. Rumor had it that "Broker money" was plentiful,[56] and both state and national Republican leaders now lent their active assistance to the unusual attempt to save the negro from unscrupulous and designing men.[57]

[53] Above, pp. 83, 99.

[54] *Landmark,* September 10 (quoting *Southern Intelligencer*).

[55] *Dispatch,* September 17, 30, October 8, 10, 14; Virginia *Star,* September 13; *Dispatch,* November 15 (quoting Cameron in New York *Herald*).

[56] *Whig,* September 30; October 10, 17, 18, 28; Northern Neck *News,* October 10; *Virginia Star,* October 29.

[57] Frederick Douglass endorsed the McCulloch Act and President Hayes

The campaign closed amid great confusion and excitement. With three sets of candidates in the field for both House and Senate (as often was the case), bargains could be made with lightning rapidity. Petersburg negroes were wild, their women urging them on, firmly believing that the McCulloch Act would "place their children in bondage for forty years to pay a debt created to hang John Brown."[58] The Funder executive committee had suggested "confidentially" that care be taken to have "one reliable person" at each voting place.[59] "Vote or die; and have your vote counted, or give short shift to those who seek to prevent," counselled the *Whig*.[60]

By a vote of 82,000 to 61,000 the Readjusters won fifty-six delegates and twenty-four senators.[61] The surprise and mortification of the Funders was intense: rascality had won; the negro was the cause; the world must know that tax payers and *real Virginians* had voted to pay the debt. In this view the outside press concurred with unusual unanimity.[62] The Readjusters

authorized Judge Hughes to telegraph his endorsement to Colonel Popham (clerk of the federal court and editor of the *Southern Intelligencer*). But the negroes considered the Douglass letter a forgery and Hayes the supplanter of Grant. The Republican state executive committee urged support of all "straight-out" Republican candidates, *Whig*, October 16, 29, 30; November 1.

[58] Petersburg *Index-Appeal*, in *Dispatch*, November 11.

[59] *Whig*, September 30.

[60] *Whig*, October 27.

[61] In the Senate, of 30 Funders, 5 were re-elected, of 13 Readjusters, 7 were re-elected and 2 replaced by other Readjusters, *Whig*, November 12. The smallness of the vote (figures are for delegates) was due to poor Funder management, the perplexity of the negro, and to the Readjusters' having no candidates in some districts (*e.g.*, Richmond) owing to lack of time and funds, *Whig*, October 30.

[62] *Dispatch*, *Whig*, Northern Neck *News*, *passim*. The New York *Tribune* was an exception.

denying all of these assertions claimed a majority of both races.

Analysis of the returns[63]—and the much larger vote of 1881 was substantially similar[64]—shows that the white and Conservative "West"[65] and the negro and Republican districts of the "East" had in the main gone Readjuster; the prevailingly Conservative and white counties of the western and northern Piedmont, Funder. The towns, even the little villages, usually went Funder;[66] the districts surrounding them, Readjuster. Several counties of the "East" distinguished from their neighbors by large white majorities and a reputation for "backwardness" were, suggestively, Readjuster.[67] The sectional, racial, and class feeling which thus appear back of the returns, were probably assisted directly by the degree of long continued economic depression; for while the map shows very mixed results, of twenty counties selected for the heaviness of realty depreciation, fourteen went Readjuster, and in only six of these did the negro predominate numerically.[68] Possibly one-fourth of the negroes and 40,000 whites, for one reason or another, left their regular parties.[69]

[63] *Cf.* maps.

[64] Seven House districts changed each way.

[65] The "Southwest" elected 18 Readjusters to 3 Funders; the Valley, 11 Readjusters to 6 Funders.

[66] Petersburg and Norfolk were Readjuster; Portsmouth, a tie. In 1881 Norfolk and Portsmouth were Funder; Danville, Readjuster.

[67] *E.g.,* Stafford, Richmond, Spottsylvania, Fairfax.

[68] The map is for the years from 1860 to 1875; for valuation in 1880, see below, p. 144. Of towns, only Petersburg and Fredericksburg showed losses.

[69] This estimate is based on a study of individual districts. *Cf. Whig, Dispatch,* November, December, *passim.* The Readjuster vote in the "West" was 23,000. In Norfolk, 169 negroes voted; the Funder white majority was 131, *Landmark,* in *Whig,* November 10, 16. From districts with a negro majority of ten per cent or more, 20 Readjusters and 12

In their local organization the Readjusters utilized the multifarious factions already existing. On the other hand, the "Funders"—as supporters of the McCulloch Act were called—controlled the old Conservative party organization, and through its central committee soon "read out" all Conservatives who opposed the McCulloch Act. Public joint-discussions characterized all stages of the campaign, the Funders appealing to "honor" and "party fidelity"; the Readjusters urging hard times and the sins of brokers and Bourbons. Late in the campaign the Readjusters bid for the negro vote, and obtained it through promises of more "rights," despite the combined efforts of the "Conservatives" and the more prominent Republicans. The election returns indicate that the Readjusters won through the combination of the negroes and the "West," aided by acute and long-continued economic distress. At best, however, the vote was light.

Funders were returned. Similar white majorities sent 28 Readjusters and 26 Funders; the rest, 10 and 4 respectively.

CHAPTER XI

NATIONAL INFLUENCES: THE READJUSTER–REPUBLICAN ALLIANCE, 1880-1881

Owing to opposition from the governor, the legislature accomplished little during the session of 1879-1880 beyond indicating with greater clearness the Readjuster program. Before this program could be completed in 1881-1882,[1] a policy in national affairs began to appear which, though in many respects not an integral part of the Readjuster Movement, gave it a national importance and profoundly modified its later course.

From 1869 to 1877 Virginia's touch with the Union had been slight. By carefully maintaining a formal obedience to reconstruction laws, the dominant Conservative party had been able to avoid serious interference from Washington, federal supervisors of elections appearing rarely, federal troops but once.[2] This was undeniably good. But the persistence with which the Republicans endeavored to regulate the domestic affairs of the South and the manifest partisanship back of it, together with the unending carping of Republican statesmen and press,[3] had naturally transformed the Demo-

[1] See ch. XII.

[2] At Petersburg, November, 1876, Governor, *Message*, December, 1876. The *Dispatch* (October 2, 1881) charged Mahone with responsibility for the conditions which led to their use.

[3] The following editorial from the New York *Times* (January 5, 1880) is by no means an extreme illustration: "'The old slave masters must domineer and tyrannize; they must keep the colored man in subjection and misery; they must raise a barrier of intolerance against enlightened

cratic preference of a majority of the whites into a fixed conviction that a decent man could under no circumstances be a Republican. Because this conviction subserved home rule by the fittest, the leaders of the Conservative party did not hesitate to foster it by every means in their power, often by language and conduct so extreme as to obscure the reasonableness of their main position.[4] Nor did the quality of the Virginia Republicans or the blindness and ineffectiveness with which they followed Grant afford any considerable correction to the excesses of this sentiment. Inevitably, therefore, the Conservative party had gradually abandoned its semi-independent position and become a branch of the national Democratic party—not so much a partner as a handmaid, faithful and unassuming.[5] No Virginian influenced either national politics or national legislation: the detested tobacco tax and the un-Virginian office-holders remained, proofs of isolation and impotence.

ideas, and fight against the incursion of those who would work for free institutions. . . . But one great change they must recognize. They can never again tyrannize over the nation. . . . The civilization of the South is of the past. . . . It must go down, and the sooner the better for the South and the better for the nation.''

[4] The following editorial from the *Enquirer* (July 3, 1877) is by no means extreme: ''What was 'treason,' 'rebellion' and 'the old secession spirit' a few years ago . . . is now 'Bourbonism.' . . . Let us glance briefly at the history of Southern 'Bourbonism.' First, What has it done for our own state? . . . A steadfast adherence to principles, an unswerving devotion to the constitution, a refusal to kiss the hand that smote us, has built up a pure government and brought us to the threshold of a new era of prosperity. Second, What has it done for the nation? It has vindicated the right to self-government. . . . It is Southern 'Bourbonism' that inspired the cry that now rings out all over the land as a warning to radicalism, 'Thus far shalt thou go and no farther.' . . . The vanished 'Rebel' has stood a bulwark against the treason of the victor.''

[5] Greeley was accepted in 1872 on account of the similarity of the Democratic-Liberal union to the Conservative party at that date. The state convention of 1876 neither expressed opinions on national issues (aside from reconstruction) nor instructed for presidential nominees.

Other states followed Virginia's method and example, and by 1876 the South was "solid" in political thought and action.[6] This solidarity, however commendable its origin may have been,[7] was objectionable alike to Liberals and to Radicals in the North: to the Radicals, because it was a victory of "Rebel Brigadiers" dangerous to both party and Union; to the Liberals, because it meant the perpetuation of sectionalism and race prejudice.[8] Accordingly, as the representative of the Liberals, President Hayes attempted in 1877 to break this solidarity by removing its more obvious causes,[9] and by offering place to Southern Democrats who would share in his administration. In Virginia conditions were not unfavorable, for *ante-bellum* leaders were largely gone and old national issues were dormant,[10] the Conservative party was overgrown and the Republican discredited, while on tariff and money questions opinion was far from being unanimous. The attempt, however, proved

[6] New York *Herald*, January 10, October 22, 1869; *Enquirer*, November 11, 1877; *Nation*, August 4, 1876, April 5, 1877; Dunning, *Reconstruction*, p. 303.

[7] *Cf. Nation*, 1869, 1873, *passim*.

[8] An additional objection was the very modern one of Southern influence in the national convention. *Cf.* Cincinnati *Gazette*, in *Dispatch*, January 1, 1879.

[9] The presence of federal troops and the active participation of federal officials in politics, Sparks, *National Development*, ch. 8; Dunning, *Reconstruction*, p. 211. The president's idea was not new, see *Dispatch, Enquirer, Landmark*, 1874, *passim*. "Assessment" of federal employees for partisan purposes seems to have been approved or tolerated by Hayes, *Annual Cyc.*, 1882, art. "Congress."

[10] The legislature and the Conservative party sought to make use of the federal treasury. Examples are: joint resolutions for an American university and an American printing-house for the blind (1870-1871), for assumption of all state debts, and for appropriation of the net public land revenue to education (1879-1880); party requests for completion of the James River and Kanawha Canal (1873); press endorsement of federal aid in the construction of the Texas Pacific Railroad (*Whig, Enquirer, passim*).

disastrous. For while the liberal "outs," largely the Mahone following,[11] maintained an open mind and possibly a receptive disposition, the other wing, to which the president made his appeal, repelled him with hot Bourbon wrath or cold partisan calculation.[12] In other Southern states the result was the same.[13]

The next attempt to detach Virginia from the solid South was due to influences that President Hayes and the independent opinion of the North would gladly have discredited. Senators Conkling, Cameron, and Logan, highly incensed at the threatened injury to the political machines, were plotting to retain the old system and restore Republican control over Congress by electing Grant for a third term.[14] In the fall of 1879, ex-Senator Simon Cameron quietly came to Richmond and made secret arrangements with Mahone. In accordance with these arrangements the Republicans of the legislature helped to elect Mahone to the federal Senate, despite the efforts of the Funders to effect a different combination.[15]

11 See *Whig, Landmark*, April, 1877, *passim*, including quotations from the Petersburg *Index-Appeal. Cf.* above, ch. 6.

12 J. L. M. Curry (above) was offered a place in the cabinet, Alderman and Gordon, *J. L. M. Curry*, ch. 14. The *Enquirer* demanded that those who took his "pay for treason" be visited with the "social terror," see February 27, March 10, 24. The *Dispatch* urged the danger of Radical rule and the possibilities of an alliance of interest with the West, see especially April 13. Dr. Curry's declination was based on grounds of broad policy.

13 *Cf.* Mayes, *Lamar*, p. 319.

14 Sparks, *National Development*, pp. 167 ff.; Cooper, *American Politics*, I, 242; Conkling, *Roscoe Conkling*, chs. 29, 30, 31; W. S. Kerr, *Senator John Sherman*, chs. 45, 46. Don Cameron, son of ex-Senator Simon Cameron, the boss of Pennsylvania, was now Senator and chairman of the Republican national committee. He was credited with originating the idea by the *Nation*, September 7, 1882.

15 Cooper, *American Politics*, I, p. 263. Mr. Cooper was chairman of the Pennsylvania state committee, a consistent Republican and a ring man. His story is confirmed by Withers, *Autobiography*, p. 386, and by contemporary suspicion, *e.g.*, New York *Times*, April 22, 1880. The Funders sup-

Soon the old rumor was revived that the Readjusters would support Grant the next year; but this rumor, as late as November 7, was branded by the *Whig* as a "stupendous falsehood."

Whether in accordance with the Cameron agreement or not, Mahone in 1880 adopted a curious and tortuous policy. He first suggested, early in the year, that the Readjusters nominate independent Congressional candidates and an independent electoral ticket, "uncommitted to any National party or its candidate, and instructed to vote together in the electoral college as may seem best to them for Virginia, for the South, and for the Union"; to which the *Whig* added the gloss that "if the vote should be close between the National parties [as in 1876], the Readjuster Electors, if elected, would be in a commanding position well worth striving for."[16] Meantime, however, the North was diligently encouraged to believe that the debt issue was but a pretext under cover of which the color line had been broken and "Bourbonism" was being overthrown;[17] and this belief was widely held, especially among the friends of Grant.[18] When, therefore, after a short but vigorous Sherman campaign,[19] Grant appeared to be the decided choice of the Virginia Republicans, Mahone deliberately advocated

ported the "Ross Hamilton" bill proposed by the negro of that name and drawn, it was said, by Congressman Dezendorf and other Republicans, *Dispatch*, February 28, 29, 1880.

[16] *Whig*, January 31; *Dispatch*, February 2, 3 (quoting Mahone interviews in Philadelphia *Press* and New York *Herald*). The *Whig* recalled the original function of electors.

[17] *Op. cit.; Dispatch*, November 15, 1879 (Cameron interview).

[18] New York *Times*, April 22, 28, July 7; New York *Tribune*, February 2, 3, April 22; *Nation*, March 3, 4, April 29.

[19] The New York *Times* (January 24, February 17) charged, giving names and places, that Sherman tried to effect fusion in the Congressional districts and to win votes for himself by extensive use of the treasury patronage. The *Tribune* denied this.

fusion on the basis of six Readjuster and five Republican electors pledged to Grant. But, despite the strategy of the party chairman,[20] and the pleas of the Lewises[21] and the *Southern Intelligencer* (hitherto Funder), the Republican convention, controlled by office-holders and guided by Gen. W. C. Wickham, Mahone's *quondam* railroad antagonist, voted fusion down, though only by a very narrow majority and after an all-night session, during which, it was said, a stampede for the Mahone fusion plan was averted only by a false fire alarm.[22] Undaunted, Mahone then called a Readjuster convention which nominated an electoral ticket pledged to Hancock;[23] and having attempted unsuccessfully to fuse this with the regular Hancock ticket, he supported it to the end.[24] None the less, the Readjuster candidates for Congress took so unhesitating a stand for the upbuilding of the material interests of the commonwealth, through protective tariffs and internal improvements at national expense, and expressed such fervent thanks that the day had come when the proud Bourbon was beneath the feet of the common white man, that the Republican national committee urged their support in several districts.[25] But the ''intense prejudice for maintaining democratic

[20] C. P. Ramsdell and James Brady, chairman and secretary respectively, published their resignation on the issue of Hayes's civil service order (above) but did not call the committee to receive it. Following the precedent afforded by the national Republican committee, they now resumed their places, and called a convention, small, early, and in the heart of the white and Readjuster Valley, *Southern Intelligencer*, December 17, 1879, January 3, 19, 1880.

[21] Ex-Senator John F. Lewis and his brother, L. L. Lewis, then federal district attorney.

[22] *Dispatch, Whig*, New York *Times*, April 23; *Nation*, April 29, 1880.

[23] *Whig, State*, New York *Times*, July 7, 8; *Nation*, July 15, 1880.

[24] *State*, October 18, 22, 28, November 1; *Nation*, October 28, November 1, 1880.

[25] *Whig*, June 5; *State*, October, November, *passim*, 1880; Address of Straight-out Republicans, 1884; *New Virginia*.

supremacy'' and the ''solid phalanx in which the colored people were marched to the polls and voted—contributed to produce consternation and a stampede.''[26] Readjusters polled only 30,000 votes for president. They maintained their organization unimpaired, however, and sent Fulkerson and Paul to the House of Representatives at Washington. ''I can not be dismayed,'' wrote Mahone, ''nor deterred from adherence to principle. . . . The duty of the hour is organization and preparation for the fight ahead.''[27]

At the special session of Congress of March, 1881, Mahone entered the Senate and by his vote gave the Republicans control over its organization.[28] The Republicans, in turn, nominated Riddleberger and George C. Gorham[29] for sergeant-at-arms and clerk of the Senate respectively, and gave Mahone the chairmanship of one committee and a commanding position on three others. These acts precipitated prolonged and vigorous discussion. Renouncing any obligation to act with the Democratic party because he had been elected as a Readjuster, Mahone declared himself still a Democrat, but utterly opposed to Bourbon control through tyranny of public opinion and suppression of the negro vote. The Democrats sought to show that the Republicans were buying help from a party traitor and repudiator. But the president sent him flowers and Senators Logan, Hoar,[30] and Cameron rushed to his defence. A speech

[26] Mahone to Harvie, November 5, 1880.

[27] *Op. cit.*

[28] *Cong. Record*, 47 Cong., Special Sess., pp. 5, 22, 33, 55, 85, 137, 176; New York *Times*, March 7, 10, 15, 16; New York *Tribune*, March 15; Mayes, *J. Q. L. Lamar*, ch. 25; Hill, *Senator B. H. Hill of Georgia;* Cooper, *American Politics*, III, p. 207.

[29] Gorham had been serviceable in securing Republican co-operation in the legislature of 1879-1880. See also below, p. 154.

[30] Yet Mr. Hoar says (*Autobiography*, II, p. 160): ''With the exception of Reverdy Johnson, of Maryland, there is no record of a single manly

of Cameron's was significant. The desire to elect Riddleberger, he said, was "something higher and above" a mere effort to reward party friends and control the organization of the Senate. It concerned the coming political contest in Virginia. It will be the best proof that could be given of the confidence which the Republican party has in all true men who uphold the laws, of its respect for them, and desire to co-operate with them. "All that we ask is that they shall stand with us in favor of securing to each lawful voter the right to cast one free and unintimidated vote, and to have it honestly counted." If this be done, "the Solid South is a thing of the past."

The campaign for governor and legislature (1881) had, indeed, already begun. Warned by the strength of Democratic sentiment displayed the year before among the Readjusters, Mahone announced in January that the maneuvers of 1880 had been merely incidental, and that the main issue would be the same as in 1879.[31] The state convention early in June reiterated this announcement, adding to the issues railroad regulation in the interest of the people and a formal condemnation of suffrage restrictions. Significantly enough, however, the convention dared to join to these democratic principles an endorsement of federal aid in the development of mining and manufacturing. The state ticket, too, presented a nicely calculated balance: "There's Cameron, he's for the Democrats; and there's Lewis, he's for the negroes; and there's Blair, he's for the Greenback lunatics," commented the *Dispatch*.[32] Then was

remonstrance, or expression of disapproval, from the lips of any prominent Southern man" against election frauds in the South. Nor does he mention Mahone in his autobiography.

[31] *Whig*, January 4, 14, 1881.

[32] June 4. For the elimination of Massey, see below, p. 152. John S. Wise was the choice of Richmond Readjusters for governor.

seen much running of Republicans to and from Washington, the result of which was that the "Coalitionist" faction endorsed the "Anti-Bourbon, or Liberal, Party," along with the payment of "every dollar [of the debt] honestly due," and the "Straight-outs" soon withdrew the ticket which recollections of the year before had induced them to put into the field without the usual authorization.[33]

The response of the Funders to these movements was significant.[34] They accepted Readjuster ideas[35] as to the schools by pledging the payment of all funds appropriated "by the constitution or otherwise." They promised "equality of right and exact justice to all men," including specifically fair elections and jury service of both races. They coupled the name of James Barbour with that of John W. Daniel on their state ticket, and agreed to use all "lawful and constitutional means in [their] power to secure the settlement of the debt upon the basis of a three per cent boud," with but one class of creditors and without increase of taxes. Having thus minimized the differences between the two factions of the old party, they rang the charge of a corrupt Republican alliance, and, as the campaign progressed, cautiously urged, under the leadership of A. M. Keiley, the re-establishment of race lines in politics. The Readjusters countered vigorously: W. E. Cameron boldly talked of carrying "Africa into the war"; federal appointments favorable to Mahone began to be reported; and soon, with the succession of Arthur to the presidency, removals took place in his interest,[36] and Senator

---

[33] For full account see *Annual Cyc.*, 1881.

[34] *Dispatch, State*, June 2, 1881. *Cf. Dispatch,* November 15, 1879. The Conservative debt plank was almost identical with that advocated by Mahone in 1879.

[35] Below, p. 160.

[36] Gorham is reported to have said in 1882 that Garfield insisted on

Cameron "passed around the hat" among the revenue officials throughout the country.[37] But the net result was a fuller vote rather than any change from the alignment of 1879; for the issues of that year had not been settled. And the victory was similar to that of 1879.

Thus, before the new and victorious party could do more than indicate clearly its program in state affairs, two external forces began to attract it toward Republicanism. These forces were the sentiment of liberalism and the exigencies of machine politicians. That the latter would determine its ultimate course was asserted by many thoughtful men. In the second contest for control of the state, however, the Readjusters won on the same issues as in the first: a larger vote indicating greater popular interest and better organization.

treating Mahone as a Republican Senator if he continued to support Republicans in the Senate, *Dispatch*, October 12, 1882. Mahone stated that he received little federal help before Arthur's administration, New York *Times*, November 20, 1881. Blaine at first opposed him. On September 22 the *Nation* said, "News has been coming in for some time that Federal officers are being removed for refusing to act with Mahone and the Readjusters," and gave specific instances. *Cf.* Sparks, *National Development*, p. 328.

[37] Cooper, *American Politics*, I, p. 264; *Nation*, June 2, 9, 16, 23, 30, August 18; *Annual Cyc.*, 1881.

CHAPTER XII

THE READJUSTERS IN POWER, 1879-1883

The period of Readjuster control over the legislature, from December, 1879, to December, 1883, proved to be a period of Readjuster supremacy in all departments. During the first two years the Readjusters were, indeed, hampered by a Funder governor, and insurgents clogged the machinery for the greater part of the last two years.[1] Some have claimed, too, that much of what was done was due to influences discussed in the preceding chapter and should be credited to "Mahoneism," not to Readjustment. None the less, a great deal was accomplished during these years, and little of it without the consent of those whom the Readjusters had freely chosen to lead them.

Of Readjuster legislation, "An act for the preservation of the credit of the state," commonly called the "Riddleberger bill,"[2] formed the very heart. Vetoed by Governor Holliday in 1880 as in flat defiance of both state and federal courts and contrary to "the spirit which has ever moved and inspired the traditions of the commonwealth,"[3] this bill was remodelled and two years later received the signature of Governor Cameron.[4] One-third of the principal and accrued interest, as of

---

[1] The governor's term began with January.

[2] In *Whig*, February 10, 1880.

[3] Sen. *Jour.*, 1879-1880, p. 440.

[4] Act of February 14, 1882. For character of amendments, see below.

July 1, 1863, was set aside for West Virginia.[5] By deducting from the remaining principal all sums paid through the sinking funds since that date, the debt principal was found to be $16,843,034. The total interest unpaid to July 1, 1863, and since accruing on the corrected principal was $25,743,268; deducting sums paid or assumed in some other form the balance of interest due was $4,192,343. The total debt (including the literary fund)[6] was therefore declared to be $21,035,-377,[7] as of July 1, 1882. New eighteen-fifty bonds, dated July 1, 1882, and bearing three per cent interest payable in lawful money, were offered in exchange for the various classes of outstanding indebtedness, the ratio of exchange being determined by subtracting from the amount of each class the interest on it already paid.[8] Payment of interest on the debt in any other form was forbidden. The new bonds became known as ''Riddle-bergers.''

As a supplement to this act, two ''coupon-killers'' had already been passed. These forbade tax collectors, under pain of heavy penalties, to receive coupons except ''for verification'' before a jury of the county and when accompanied by the amount of the taxes in cash; upon the establishment of their genuineness the cash would be refunded. The remedy offered for the breach of contract[9] would, it was thought, satisfy the courts; the difficulty and cost of proving the genuineness of coupons, clipped from bonds held abroad perhaps, would prevent

[5] West Virginia entered the Union June 20, 1863. Certificates of indebtedness ''to be accounted for by the state of West Virginia, without recourse upon this commonwealth'' were given.

[6] Principal, $1,428,245; interest, $602,016, Second Auditor, *Report,* 1881.

[7] Approximately, a scaling of ten millions.

[8] Consols would exchange at 53, ten-forties at 60, peelers at 69, etc.

[9] Above, p. 43.

their deluging the treasury and tend to encourage conversion of consols and ten-forties into Riddlebergers.[10]
Thus the long-desired uniformity and definiteness of
obligations, and an adequate reduction in the annual
interest burden, seemed assured for the not distant
future.

While readjusting the debt, the legislature also began
a readjustment of taxation. In this matter, the wretch-
edness of the existing system might well have authorized
a thoroughgoing revision. No more serious purpose
appears to have been entertained, however, than to
lighten for the time the burden of the laborer and the
farmer, and to gain some partisan advantage thereby.
Thus the new measures declared that the poll tax need
no longer be paid before voting, substituted the older
and lighter liquor license plan for the Moffett law,[11]
reduced the tax rate on general property from fifty to
forty cents, and ordered a reassessment of realty under
conditions which resulted in a diminution of $13,000,-
000.[12] To offset the loss in revenue thus entailed, an
effort was made to reach corporate wealth; and this
effort, it should be recorded, was serious and eventually
successful.[13] The energetic measures taken to collect
delinquent taxes, to compel county treasurers or their

[10] Acts of January 14 and January 26, 1882. See above, pp. 42, 65,
for origin of this method of attack.

[11] Above, p. 57; *Acts*, 1879-1880, p. 147. Fulkerson introduced the
bill at the request of the liquor dealers, *Whig*, January 16, 1880.

[12] *Acts*, 1881-1882, p. 497. The old plan was used, but by Readjuster
appointees and with extended opportunities for local revision, *cf.* above,
p. 91.

[13] *Cf.* above, p. 56, [Douglas S. Freeman], *Report of the Virginia Tax
Commission* (1911), appendix, ch. 6; Magruder, *Recent Administration*,
p. 175. The taxable value of railroads in 1880 was $9,876,000; in 1885,
$35,955,000.

sureties to settle,[14] and to adjust old claims of the state against the railroads[15] were of similar importance, for they enabled the Readjusters to punish enemies and reward friends, and produced a temporary abundance of funds. These funds the legislature proceeded to spend with an abandon but little short of recklessness.[16]

The direction which the liberality of the legislature took was significant. Public education received such generous treatment that some feared the ruin of the denominational schools.[17] The Riddleberger act put the literary fund in the most favored class of creditors and directed that the interest in arrears be paid in cash to the amount of $378,000. The state tax rate for schools was not reduced; local boards were authorized to tax railroad and telegraph property for their support; and, under the "Granstaff" act, the percentage of the schools' estimated quota of state taxes to be retained by local authorities was increased to ninety.[18] The full claim of the schools to taxes previously "diverted" was admitted, and regular quarterly payments of $25,000 and

[14] Auditor, *Reports*, 1880, 1881; *Acts*, 1879-1880, pp. 74, 136, 293, 299.

[15] *Acts*, 1881-1882, pp. 76, 400, 490. Thus ended the state's ownership in railroads, with the exception of the R. F. & P. stock, which is still retained and is exceedingly profitable, and some minor properties sold in 1882-1883. The A. M. & O. sale (below) was generally conceded a good bargain for the state. The Richmond and Danville was permitted to redeem an amply secured debt of $420,000, due four years later, with "Riddlebergers" worth about 50. The requirement that this road surrender its exemption from taxation appears to have been a condition attached to the issue of new stock, and not a part of the sales bargain.

[16] For contemporary discussion of wastefulness from the Readjuster standpoint, see the reply of John S. Wise to Holmes Conrad, in *Whig*, September 25, 1883. At that date the treasury contained one and one-half millions.

[17] Richmond *Christian Advocate*, January 26, 1882. Colleges were given special privileges later, *Acts*, 1881-1882, p. 203.

[18] *Cf.* above, p. 87; *Acts*, 1881-1882, pp. 166, 203, 233.

a special payment of $400,000 thereon were directed.[19] This $400,000 was secured from the settlement of the A. M. & O. claims. The remaining $100,000, derived from the same source, was granted, together with a fixed annuity, to a negro ''Normal and Collegiate Institute,''[20] the construction and operation of which were quickly begun. Altogether, public schools received from the state annually about $600,000, as against less than $400,000 annually from 1870 to 1877.[21] For lunatic asylums approximately $250,000 a year was spent, as compared with $190,000 in 1879 (when special attention had been given them), and a new building for the colored insane was virtually completed.[22] Nor did the maimed Confederate soldier lose any part of his customary paltry donation.[23]

If this legislation, while primarily fiscal, had an important social significance, still more did a multitude of other measures, passed or nearly passed, tend to subserve the interests of the masses and to break the power of wealth and established privilege.[24] The poll tax, imposed originally for the benefit of schools which should train citizens to vote but converted by Bourbons and debt payers into a restriction on suffrage, was repealed.[25]

[19] Cf. above, p. 62; Acts, 1881-1882, pp. 203, 473.

[20] Ibid., p. 286. Apparently this money should have been used to reduce the debt. Above, p. 19.

[21] Auditor, Reports, 1877, 1880 to 1883. The estimates are the author's.

[22] Auditor, Reports; reports of asylums, in Annual Reports, 1884; Acts, 1881-1882, p. 246. The new asylum had been long projected. The Southwestern Asylum (white) might be credited to Readjuster influence, Acts, 1883-1884, p. 692.

[23] Auditor, Reports, passim. The total average annual payment was about $10,000. It had been very irregularly made.

[24] There is an excellent, though partisan, summary by B. B. Munford in State, September 13, 1889.

[25] Funders aided in the final stages from party motives and because of

The whipping-post was abolished; mechanics were better secured in their wages; foreign insurance companies were put under a stricter bond;[26] and benevolent and fraternal organizations were chartered by the score, among them a "Labor Association of Lynchburg." N. W. Hazelwood, in behalf of the state grange, championed bills to prevent fraud in the manufacture of fertilizers, to establish experiment stations, to provide state supervision over the warehousing and sampling of tobacco, and to regulate the rates and management of the railroads.[27] Lady pushed a commissioner-of-sales bill which would have transferred the management of property to be sold under judicial decree from the supposedly grasping lawyers to special state officials. Heretofore, especially in 1877-1879, the legislature had gladly removed disabilities incurred for duelling; henceforth, state officials must make oath that they would never participate, directly or indirectly, in this relic of past customs.[28]

The state administrative departments, wrote Massey, just after the victory of 1879, must be put "in sympathy with the people." "If I can exert any influence," declared Mahone, "not one of them [the present officials] shall go unexpelled—and that quickly."[29] In this view the

the corruption to which it gave rise, see below, p. 156; *Whig*, January 23, 1880, September 25, 1883 (John S. Wise); *Dispatch*, April 7; *State*, April 22, 1882. Fulkerson was patron of the repeal. The vote on ratification was 107,303, to 66,131.

[26] *Acts*, 1879-1880, pp. 81, 87.

[27] *House Bills*, 1881-1882. Hazlewood was secretary of the grange and a member of the legislature. Duff Green presented the railroad bill. For ulterior purpose, see below, p. 158.

[28] *Acts*, 1881-1882, p. 404. Hazlewood favored a more extreme measure, *House Bills*, 1881-1882, No. 207.

[29] Letters to Colonel Harvie, November 10, 11, 1879, *Harvie Papers*. For method of selecting officials see below.

legislature unanimously concurred. By common consent Massey became auditor. The energy and ability which he brought to this important office, long slothfully and incompetently administered by an appointee of Governor Peirpoint, justified the selection.[30] His successor, S. Brown Allen, however, was a "Mahone man," and proved an entirely unsatisfactory official. A scheme devised by Massey for the collection of delinquent taxes became in the hands of both, but especially of Allen, a powerful and sometimes corrupting political asset.[31] C. M. Reynolds and T. T. Fauntleroy, "original readjusters," received the easy places of treasurer and secretary of the commonwealth. They served acceptably[32] until 1882, when they were replaced by the "Mahone men," D. R. Reverly and W. C. Elam. Gen. Asa Rogers, long second auditor and as such directly in charge of the debt and the school funds, became railroad commissioner, and H. H. Dyson, a Republican, took his place. Despite the protests of even Republican friends of public education, Superintendent Ruffner was replaced at the end of his term by R. R. Farr—a severely ironic commentary upon the sincerity or the intelligence of Readjuster interest in the schools.[33]

With startling directness the legislature declared vacant the controlling boards of the several state asylums and colleges; and in some instances even ven-

[30] Massey, *Autobiography*, ch. 15; House *Jour.*, 1881-1882, December 16; comparison of auditors' reports. Auditor Taylor was in large part the victim of circumstances.

[31] Sen. *Jour.*, 1883-1884, Docs. 27, 30; House *Jour.*, 1883-1884 and 1884, Index.

[32] Sen. *Jour.*, 1881-1882, Doc. 20. The selection of Fauntleroy was criticised by the *Dispatch*, which had previously commended him.

[33] Massey, *Autobiography*, p. 204; Ruffin, *Mahoneism;* House *Jour.*, 1883-1884, Index; *Ruffner Papers* (letters of Gen. S. C. Armstrong, president of the Hampton School, to Ruffner, 1881).

tured to order an immediate reorganization of the institution affected.[34]   For this the general excuse was "Bourbon" inefficiency and lack of sympathy with the masses.
There was truth in the charge; but under the new
régime the improvement in efficiency was not as notice-
able as the amount of petty extravagance and humiliat-
ing partisanship.[35]   So, too, the old county and city
school superintendents, who had been selected mainly
because of their moral and scholastic qualifications, were
largely replaced by men of energy in close "touch with
the people."   But as the new appointees used their
energies primarily in the service of the party and the
superintendent and the county judge controlled the local
boards of school trustees, which selected the teachers,
the entire school system began to feel, what had been so
long feared, the vicious influence of politics unabashed.[36]

Nor were the courts spared.   For a century they had
been citadels of conservatism and respectability.   They
were wont to be affected by politics only remotely.   Because of the character of the judges, extra-judicial
powers had been given them in matters requiring impartial and scrupulously honest attention, such as the
appointment of election officials and assessors and the
selection of school trustees.   Most of them, however, held
Funder views; besides, Readjusters needed the power
and prestige of their offices.   So the legislature retired
all of the supreme court judges and about three-fourths
of the county and corporation judges as their terms
expired, and was with difficulty prevented from vacating
the circuit courts under the pretense of redistricting.
The new supreme court judges served full terms without

[34] *Acts,* March 9, 1880; February 15, March 3, April 7, 14, 1882.

[35] Reports of superintendents and boards in *Annual Reports;* Sen. *Jour.*,
1883-1884, Docs. 32, 33.

[36] Sen. and House *Journals,* 1881-1882, Index; below, p. 167.

discredit. But the scarcity of Readjuster lawyers, party exigencies, and the refusal of some Funder lawyers to accept Readjuster appointment led to many unsatisfactory and some scandalous selections. By 1884, six appointees had resigned under pressure, one had been removed, and six had died. In the opinion of some competent observers, no other action of the Readjusters produced such deep dissatisfaction as did this.[37]

That the legislature sent self-made men to the national senate was perhaps accidental. Through their energy and their willingness to exchange deciding votes for federal patronage, however, these Senators gave to Virginia a prominence and an influence which she had not possessed for more than a generation. Neither Mahone nor Riddleberger spoke frequently, being immersed in state politics most of the time. Both advocated a high protective tariff, Mahone having much to do with the notorious iron schedule in the Tariff Act of 1883. Both advocated liberalism, Mahone to the extent of vilifying a large part of his constituents. But in neither of these positive attitudes did they represent the most intelligent and substantial citizens of their state or rise to the level of national statesmanship.[38]

[37] Massey, *Autobiography*, p. 217; Senate and House *Journals*, 1879-1880, 1881-1882, 1883-1884, Index; *Whig* and *Dispatch, passim;* Royall, *Virginia State Debt Controversy*, ch. 5. Convenient lists may be found in the *Warrock-Richardson Almanack*. Supreme court judges were: Robert A. Richardson, T. T. Fauntleroy, L. L. Lewis (below), B. W. Lacy, D. A. Hinton. Prominent among county judges not removed were John W. Bell, Jos. H. Sherrard, William H. Mann. Prominent new appointees were J. R. McDaniel, Jas. M. Gregory, Edmund Waddill, F. S. C. Hunter, William R. Taliaferro, A. M. Lybrook, Robert Mayo. Prominent as corporation judges were Thos. S. Atkins, A. C. Holliday, D. J. Godwin, N. B. Meade, S. B. French. That some were illegally retired was strongly maintained.

[38] Above, p. 138. Mahone voted on but 7 of the 22 matters deemed worthy of a recorded vote by the *Annual Cyc.* He was one of the conferees, "placed there at a late hour," who raised the duty on iron ore from 50 to 75 cents, *Annual Cyc.*, 1883, art. "Congress."

If one views the legislation of this period as a whole, its resemblances to the ultra-democratic ideas imbedded in the constitution is at once apparent. So, too, the comparative absence of well-known names among the holders of office and the prominence of hitherto obscure men bring to mind the carpet-bagger and scalawag régime. One striking exception, however, presents itself, and that is the attitude toward the negro. Though the needs and wishes of the freedmen now had much more weight than during the preceding decade, no effort was made to "elevate" them by special legislation. Even the election laws remain unchanged. Appointment to office they did indeed receive, but only as "our faithful allies" and never very frequently.[39] If a second democratic revolution was in truth under way, the forces controlling it were the farmers and the poor whites and the aspiring middle class leaders.

Both the rapidity of legislation and the character and activities of appointees were largely due to the authority exercised by General Mahone. The Readjusters had, in fact, been developing a "machine," of which Mahone was by 1882 the absolute "boss."[40]

The stages of this development are clear. The convention of 1879[41] lodged party control in a state committee representative of the Congressional district delegations. The legislative caucus that followed emphasized this oligarchical tendency by apportioning the state patronage to the Congressional districts, the positions to be

[39] Below, p. 163.

[40] "A member of the Legislature" [Holmes Conrad], *Mahoneism Unveiled,* in Ruffin, *Scrap-Book,* II (originally published in the Winchester *Times,* 1883); A. M. Lybrook's letter in *Dispatch,* September 12, 1882; Ruffin, *Mahoneism Unveiled* and *An Appeal;* Munford's letter in *State,* September 13, 1889. *Cf.* Massey, *Autobiography,* ch. 17.

[41] Above, p. 101.

filled on nomination by the legislators therefrom.[42] Thus
a corps of leaders, salaried and uniformly distributed,
was assured. As the single chairman of the party, however, as well as its most distinguished member and the
owner of the *Whig,* Mahone from the first exercised
unusual influence, to which was added early in 1880 the
prestige of a United States Senator-elect. To him, therefore, was generally conceded the task of "talking over"
those who were dissatisfied with the action of the "committee on spoils," as the caucus apportionment committee was aptly termed; and from this fact it is reasonable to infer that he was consulted in advance of the
apportionment. But thus far the authority which he
wielded was only such as any capable leader might
obtain and was perhaps little greater than that enjoyed
by "Parson" Massey, "the most popular man in the
party." After his successful début in the Senate, however, Mahone advanced by bold and rapid strides to
complete control. First, by clever manipulation of the
state convention, he secured the defeat of Massey's
gubernatorial aspirations, and thereby sidetracked his
only rival. Then, strengthened by this victory and by
the open and vigorous support of President Arthur, he
quietly obtained from the candidates for the legislature
a written "pledge," "under seal," to "stand by the
Readjuster party" and to go into the party caucus and

---

[42] Fulkerson presided. Massey, who had been defeated, was made an
honorary member. Judge B. W. Lacy, of New Kent, became speaker, and
P. H. McCaul, clerk of the House; Gen. W. M. Elliott became president
pro tem., and C. H. Causey, of Nansemond, clerk of the Senate; A. J.
Taylor and C. M. Webber (editor of the Salem *Register*) became sergeants-
at-arms. Riddleberger and Paul were active in patronage arrangements.
Much to their annoyance, the *Dispatch* managed to report these meetings
quite fully.

abide by its results.[43]   After the elections, in a preliminary conference of leaders selected by himself, the work of the legislature was mapped out; and, when the legislature assembled, this program was gradually unfolded for adoption in the caucus under rules of procedure which its members were bluffed into accepting, and which, some of them asserted, they were not allowed even to read. The revolt followed of the "Big Four," as four members of the caucus who had not given the pledge came to be called;[44] and as a result of this revolt most of the measures objectionable to even a few Readjuster legislators failed of passage.   But the "Big Four" and their backers were quickly "read out of the party."   Nor was Mahone's supremacy questioned again for two years.

This machine, as has been suggested above, rested

[43] Lybrook, *op. cit.*   The procedure followed in obtaining the pledge is illustrative of Mahone's indirect methods.   The "Judge" addressed below was Lybrook.   "Fernald" was the Republican collector of internal revenue at Danville.

"U. S. Internal Revenue Office,
Danville, Va., Sept. 14, 1881.

Dear Judge.—I send you herewith two 'pledges' to sign one and have the party nominee for your county to sign the other one, and return to me, and I will forward them to Gen. Mahone, *who directs me to do this.*

Of course it is nothing for an honest man to do and sign his hand to his faith.   Please attend to this promptly.

Fernald."

"Patrick Co., Virginia,
.... 1881.

"I hereby pledge myself to stand by the Readjuster party and platform, and to go into caucus with the Readjuster members of the Legislature, and vote for all measures, nominees and candidates to be elected by the Legislature that meets in Richmond, as the caucus may agree upon.

Given under my hand and seal this .... day of Sept., A. D., 1881."

[44] Senators S. H. Newberry, of Bland, and P. G. Hale, of Grayson, formerly Conservatives, and A. M. Lybrook, of Patrick, and B. F. Williams, of Nottoway, formerly Republicans.   It is the popular opinion in Virginia that these men saved the day.

primarily upon its control over the patronage, state and national. The extent of state patronage has already been indicated.[45] Equally important was the national patronage. In round numbers, the treasury service employed two hundred men at an annual salary of $400,000, the post-office department, 1,700 postmasters at $150,000. Connected with the federal courts were some seventy men.[46] The navy yard at Portsmouth was a large and unfailing employer at critical times. In the prevailing scarcity of money and dearth of business enthusiasm, these positions were all deemed highly desirable, and therefore worth working for. Moreover, their holders could be "assessed" regularly and with confidence. So, too, could Virginia's quota of the employees in Washington.[47] And to these sources of strength should be added the sympathetic support of the *National Republican,* of Washington, under the editorship of Gorham and Assistant Postmaster General Hatton.[48]

A second reason for the facility with which Mahone established machine control is found not so much in the character of the Readjuster leaders or in the enthusiasm which their plans aroused, though each of these was contributory, as in the possession of the negro vote. Trained by the slave system to unquestioning obedience, the colored men had easily learned to follow political bosses during reconstruction days. Being gregarious by instinct, they almost always moved *en masse.* And since their ignorance was stupendous and their credulity childlike, flattery, bribery, and threats were sufficient

[45] Above.

[46] *Register of U. S. Officials,* 1879.

[47] New York *Herald,* in *Dispatch,* October 22, 1882.

[48] Above, p. 138; New York *Tribune,* June 5, 1883. Hatton was later postmaster general.

to win them—one was under no necessity of inventing a
reason for the course they were advised to take.[49] There
were, indeed, important offsets to these advantages:
their inability to move without white leadership, for
example, and the perpetual danger of provoking a recru-
descence of race politics. But these disadvantages did
not become operative until 1883.

The manner in which Mahone used his control over
the machine is striking. Indeed, in the opinion of some
it constituted the most important phase of the Readjuster movement. Illustrations abound. Thus, despite
the pledges of two state conventions, the Riddleberger
Act was not submitted to the people, nor did it directly
repudiate war and reconstruction interest on the debt,
both of which the Republicans of the North thought
unwise.[50] To gerrymander Congressional districts even
to the extent of making 187,000 people in a white district
equivalent to 132,000 in a black district was perhaps not
unusual; but to avow the partisan motive and to express
open regret that only eight "administration" representatives could be thus assured was rather startling.[51]
The second mortgage bond which Mahone himself had
executed as president of the A. M. & O. he induced the

[49] The following was printed by the *Dispatch* as a speech of W. L.
Fernald delivered at Halifax Court House: "It does those Funder overseers so much good to see a *nigger's* back whipped. Every time they see
a nigger's back cut, they jump up and clap their heels together like game
cocks. . . . You will see colored judges and lawyers in that court house,
and you will have good schools if the Readjusters succeed. . . . When a
colored man comes out against the Readjuster party, he has sold himself.
A man who goes against his race and color is *a damned scoundrel*. . . .
Some will say, what will become of the Republican party if we all go over
to the Readjusters? There is nothing in a name except the smell. . . .
My office looks Africa because I have so many colored people in it."

[50] The terms of the debt settlement are, however, in the author's opinion,
substantially the same as those of the first Riddleberger bill, which were
endorsed by the people in the election of 1881.

[51] The *Whig's* utterances are referred to.

board of public works to compromise for $500,000 in cash, and the legislature ratified the arrangement, as the schools needed the money.[52] Two bank note companies, the American and the Kendall, bid for the printing of "Riddlebergers"; the legislature awarded the contract to the lower bidder, but the other contributed $5,000 to the campaign fund and the legislature had to change its decision.[53] During President Arthur's administration some two hundred federal appointments were changed at Mahone's request;[54] fear controlled the rest. With entire openness, state employees resident in Richmond were "assessed" for campaign purposes at five per cent of their annual salary; federal employees, indirectly, at two per cent of theirs. The auditor appointed collectors of delinquent taxes with power to name their own deputies. To these collectors, receipts for the payment of the poll tax were sent, signed in blank. The Readjuster voter was handed a receipt as he entered the booth and, in 1882, federal supervisors of elections guaranteed its acceptance as a prerequisite for voting. Such voters were supposed to return the receipts; but the collector was not always bonded, and did not always render an account to the auditor.[55]

Party leaders Mahone paid well: negroes in the Norfolk region received from $300 to $500 each; men of a higher type were rewarded with public favors not always of an unquestionable character.[56] Activity was

[52] Above.

[53] *Dispatch, State,* April, 1882. The state was forced to pay the Kendall Company also. In 1885 the second auditor bought the rejected bonds at auction from an express company for $17.75, Sen. *Jour.,* 1885-1886, Doc. 10.

[54] Estimate in "New Virginia," in *Whig,* March 28, 1885.

[55] Above; Sen. *Jour.,* 1883-1884, Doc. 27; contested election cases of O'Ferrall *v.* Paul (House Misc. Docs., 48 Cong., 1 Sess., No. 16), and Massey *v.* Wise (*ibid.,* No. 2*i,* pts. 1 and 2); O'Ferrall, *Forty Years.*

[56] Ex-Congressman Dezendorf to D. B. Eaton, in New York *Tribune,*

demanded of all office-holders. Thus, the superintendent of an insane asylum not only distributed poll tax receipts but also bought the institution's provisions and used its teams in the interest of the party;[57] and the Norfolk postmaster and his assistant were reported to be usually away on party business.[58] Mahone bossed rather than guided: men said that he went into the auditor's office and appointed or removed tax collectors as if the auditor were his absent clerk; the sheriff of Pittsylvania made affidavit that Mahone telegraphed his removal;[59] Col. Frank G. Ruffin, long a "power" in the Conservative party and a staunch supporter of coalition, for protesting against assessment and the "pledge" lost his clerkship.[60] Massey alleges[61] that the gubernatorial nomination was offered him on the condition of absolute obedience to Mahone, such as Wise and Cameron had promised. Conventions usually merely registered his will: that of 1881 adopted a platform which he had sent the day before to Wall Street;[62] in 1884, having named the temporary chairman and, through him, the permanent chairman, Mahone reported from a single committee a plan of party organization, a platform, delegates to the national convention, and electors—all of which the convention ratified.[63]

Not content with this power, Mahone contemplated vast extensions and a greater concentration of the

May 14, 1883. Dezendorf was anti-Mahone; John Goode calls him "able." For favors see Ruffin, *Scrap-Book*, II, p. 174; Munford, *op. cit.*

[57] Unanimous report of bi-partisan committee, Sen. *Jour.*, 1883-1884, Docs. 32, 33.

[58] Dezendorf, *op. cit.*

[59] *Dispatch*, February 8, 1883.

[60] *Ibid.*, July 6, 9, 1882.

[61] *Autobiography*, ch. 17.

[62] *Dispatch*, June 8, 1881.

[63] *Ibid.*, April 24, 1884. Col. William Lamb was temporary chairman, Brown Allen permanent chairman.

state patronage. Of this purpose the measures defeated by the "Big Four"[64] give ample proof. To concentrate patronage was one of the aims of the bill creating the office of commissioner of sales in each county and giving him the power virtually of controlling the local newspaper through the advertising business of the office.[65] Such, too, would have been the result of the attempt to create a railroad commission with power not only to examine all books, papers, and employees, and to make rates and enforce them, but also to dismiss for cause any officer or employee.[66] These proposed offices were to be filled, not by popular election or even by legislative election, but by the governor.[67] Similarly, although the district school trustees were already under Readjuster control through their election by local boards on which Readjusters had an appointive majority, none the less an effort was made to transfer their selection to the state board of education, the members of which all held office in Richmond. Rumor had it that the sheriffs, too, now elective and the most important of the county officers, would soon be named at the state capitol. According to Colonel Ruffin, if these attempts had succeeded, 42,620 adults, drawing $18,300,000 yearly, would have become virtually subject to Mahone.

This concentration of power and its further extension Mahone and those closest to him defended, by insisting that it was necessary to break up the "rings" and to keep them broken in order that "Bourbon Democrats and Bourbon Republicans" might be overthrown and the "regeneration of Virginia" accomplished. And such

[64] Above.

[65] *House Bills*, 1881-1882, No. 259. The newspaper provision does not appear in this bill in its first form.

[66] *Ibid.*, No. 121.

[67] *Scrap-Book*, II, p. 174. Sheriffs are not included.

reasoning undoubtedly had its weight, especially at first. But the written evidence, supported by a well-defined tradition among both Democrats and Republicans today, indicates clearly that the main object of Mahone's ambition was to perpetuate the power of the machine and that this was deemed a sufficient end in itself.

What, then, are the significant features of the Readjuster period of control? On the one hand, an attempt at democratization through legislation and appointments; on the other, the development of a new political machine. The legislation was mostly economic and social, intended to subserve the interests of the masses and to break the power of the privileged classes. Much of it was progressive and sound, in line with the best tendencies of the reconstruction period. That it involved repudiation was unfortunate but probably necessary in view of the position taken by the preferred creditors. In appointments, the balance of opportunity between well-known and unknown men was redressed; even the negroes received recognition. But if the conception of offices as "honors" was dead, that of office as opportunity for public service had not been attained; instead, men served the party. That the organization of the party quickly became a machine was due in part to the circumstances of its origin and its possession of the negro vote; in part, to the skill of General Mahone and his control of the federal patronage. As the machine became perfected, it shaped both appointments and legislation more and more to suit its own ends, until it became a very real and a very debasing tyranny.

CHAPTER XIII

THE END OF READJUSTMENT, 1883-1885

With 1882 the character of Readjuster legislation and appointments ceased to be a topic of prime political interest. To put Virginia in the Republican column was now clearly Mahone's chief object; to "redeem the state" gradually became the single aim of the Conservative management. In the struggle Readjuster ideas and tactics were taken over by the victorious Conservatives, soon called Democrats, and thus they survived. Simultaneously the improvement in economic conditions became apparent.

The story need not detain us long. In April, 1882, as the spokesman of the anti-Mahone Readjusters, Massey began to "lay the matter before the people" in characteristic fashion.[1] His chief contention was that the legitimate work of the Readjuster party had been accomplished and that Mahone's purpose now was to "bind the state and hand her over to the Republicans." Others, including Fulkerson, followed. But the regularly constituted Funder leaders in Virginia were in no position to profit by this diversion—their personal interests were too closely involved, their knowledge of the inner workings of the Readjusters too intimate for

[1] Above, p. 152; Massey, *Autobiography*, chs. 17 to 20; "A. Fulkerson's Account of his Stewardship as a Congressman delivered at Abingdon," in *Fulkerson Papers;* addresses of the "Big Four" and the "Readjuster Members of the Legislature" (*cf.* Lybrook on the accuracy of this claim to authorship) in *Annual Cyc.*, 1882; Lybrook, *Mahoneism;* Ruffin, *An Appeal.*

a broad and statesmanlike view. Remote from the
cauldron of Richmond politics, however, the Democratic
leaders in Washington saw the opportunity. Quietly
seizing the party reins, they encouraged Massey to
become an independent candidate for Congressman-at-
large and then induced the state committee to give their
action a passive endorsement. Likewise, under the same
influences, several Congressional districts informally
adopted conciliatory policies. But the breach in the old
party's ranks proved too wide and the workings of the
Mahone-Republican machine too powerful, for such
spontaneous and irregular methods. Though it was a
"Democratic year," the "Coalitionists" won five of the
eight districts, and Wise defeated Massey by 5,000 votes
in a total of 193,000 cast. With Mahone in the Senate
and Riddleberger about to join him there, the "Solid
South" was unmistakably broken. This result was
attained by a combination of boss, patronage, and
negroes—a combination that might easily be effected in
almost any Southern state.[2]

With spirits thoroughly chastened by successive defeats, Funder congressmen, press, and local leaders
now, for the first time, deliberately went to the rank
and file for advice. In the widespread discussion that
ensued a Conservative policy was gradually shaped for
use in the legislative campaign of 1883: first of all, an
unequivocal and formal renunciation of the Funder
claim to a monopoly of Conservatism; secondly, a revivi-
fying of the issue by which warring factions had so long

[2] Cf. ch. 11. Throughout the South, wrote "Vates" in the Boston *Post*
(*Whig*, July 4), the negroes and the bosses are coming together, and "the
hour is big with fate." The *Nation* thought the movement "likely to
spread through the South," January 12, May 25. The *Dispatch* feared
(July 12) Mahone's success "will give such an impetus to the Coalition
movement that the arrest of that movement between now and 1884 may
be impossible."

been held together; and, thirdly, a new leadership which should be at once popular and efficient. Accordingly, the state committee early in the year agreed to call a state convention and named as the place, not Richmond, but Staunton, in the heart of the white and Readjuster Valley. In the election of delegates to this convention, the committee announced, "all Conservative Democrats are equally entitled to participate."[3] Fortune aided the venture. For in March came the decision of the highest federal court sustaining "Coupon-Killer, Number One" and thereby the Readjuster debt settlement.[4] Some Funders, indeed, to whom the decision was almost incredible, sought loopholes in the rather confused reasoning of the court; but others welcomed the opportunity for an honorable retreat, and soon the great majority declared the matter ended.[5] Satisfied, many Readjusters now entered the convention and shared its honors with their old, but hitherto preferred, party friends. The platform, formally accepting the Readjuster settlement, rang the emphasis upon "Mahoneism"; and upon the walls of the convention hall one could read "THIS WAY, FREEMEN!" With a word of praise the old leaders were set aside, and a complete reorganization after the Mahone model was

[3] "What Fulkerson did for a convention," manuscript in the hand-writing of Colonel Fulkerson, *Fulkerson Papers; Dispatch*, February 15.

[4] Antoni *v.* Greenhow, 17 U. S. Rep. 769; *Annual Cyc.*, 1883, Art. "Obligation of Contracts"; Royall, *Virginia Debt Controversy*, ch. 6. The grounds were that the remedy offered by the state for breach of contract was "substantially equivalent to that in force when the coupons were issued," and that this remedy was the "one which the state has chosen to give, and the only one therefore, which the courts of the United States are authorized to administer." Chief Justice Waite rested his decision on the first named ground, Justice Matthews on the second, Justices Bradley, Woods, and Gray concurred in both. Justices Field and Harlan dissented.

[5] *Dispatch*, March 6; *Dispatch* and *State, passim* (citations). That a belief in a conspiracy between Mahone and the Republican justices had weight (Royall, *op. cit.*) is not evident from the Richmond press.

planned. To the chairmanship of the party, with its enlarged powers and duties, the convention unanimously elected John S. Barbour, a railroad man and a Funder, but one of those who had inspired and directed the new party policy. Before the convention Barbour stated that he "didn't believe much in still-hunting with a brass band, nor had he much faith in committees. Nor in platforms." In token of the burying of old issues the name "Democrat" was now, for the first time, formally taken.[6]

Despite the consequent Democratic enthusiasm and activity,[7] however, the result of the campaign was still in doubt when the "Danville riot" gave to the Democrats a most convincing argument for the overthrow of Mahoneism.[8] The circumstances were these: Early in 1883, Governor Cameron appointed two negroes as school trustees in Richmond, and negro mass-meetings endorsed the act.[9] Many Conservatives thereupon urged that race lines be drawn. To this, however, many, especially of the ex-Readjuster following, would not consent.[10]

[6] *Dispatch, State, Whig*, July 25, 26; above, p. 101; *Dispatch*, July 28; *Whig*, November 7. Barbour was a brother of James Barbour, above, p. 111.

[7] The Democrats were aided by the opposition of Straight-outs. Mahone was handicapped by the desertion of lieutenants, see letters of Congressman Dezendorf, also editorials, in New York *Tribune*, May 14 ff.; also interview of Mahone in same, June 8. Apparently Mahone had to threaten Arthur with the loss of Virginia's vote in the national Republican convention next year, *ibid.*, June 5, 13.

[8] *Dispatch* and *Whig*, November 3-9; "*New Virginia*"; O'Ferrall, *Forty Years*, p. 294; "Personal Recollections." O'Ferrall gives the year as 1885.

[9] *Dispatch*, May, June, July, *passim*. Another negro trustee had been appointed in Lunenburg by Cameron, *State*, March 8. Kemper had done the same, *Whig*, October 3. But "Africanization" was not feared under him.

[10] Opposition to drawing the color line was greatest in the Norfolk region, where "fusion" had already begun. Many favored support of negro schools from funds contributed by negroes only.

But as the campaign grew warmer, the Democrats resorted to "dividing the crowd" on public occasions, and in many places the negroes were wrought up to a state of extreme excitement by the speeches of Republican leaders. A climax was reached in Danville. In this little "Southside" town, the whites paid $38,000 of the $40,000 taxes. But the negroes were in a majority and, aided by a new town charter which they had obtained from the "pledged" legislature, they secured a majority of the council, over which a carpet-bagger presided. All the justices of the peace, four of the nine policemen, the health officer, the weigh-master and the clerk of the market, together with twenty of the twenty-four renters of stalls in the market, were negroes. It was just such an "Africanization" as had been feared in Reconstruction days, and predicted time and again as the necessary outcome of Mahoneism. On the Saturday night preceding election day (Tuesday), a street brawl led to a "riot," in which a few whites and blacks were killed. The governor called out the militia and order was soon restored. But forthwith flaming posters told the story to the whites of the "Southwest"; and in Lynchburg a mass-meeting unanimously resolved, upon motion of the stern old Bourbon, Gen. Jubal A. Early, that "the negroes must know that they are to behave themselves and keep in their proper places." After this the result of the election was no longer in doubt. The whites turned out as never before, and the Democrats, by a majority of 18,000 in 267,000 counted, won nearly two-thirds of both houses. From all over the South came congratulations, the sincerity of which no one denied.[11]

[11] Two hundred and sixty-seven thousand votes were counted in 1883; 193,000 in 1882; 213,000 in 1881. The Democratic majority was 18,000 as against a Republican majority of 13,000 in 1881 and 5,000 in 1882.

The legislature thus elected quickly demonstrated how completely the old debt issue had ceased to be a matter of political importance. Recalling how for thirteen years this question had "profoundly agitated the people of Virginia . . . resulting in political contests which have convulsed the popular mind, given repeated and ruinous shocks to the business interests of the state, retarded prosperity, and threatened the safety of the people"; how a "large body of the citizens and tax-payers" had made "persistent, repeated, and earnest but unavailing efforts to effect and carry out a settlement, by which a much larger sum would have been recognized and assumed by the state than has been assumed by the 'Riddleberger Bill' ' "; and how the people had endorsed this bill at three successive elections and the highest courts had declared it valid, the legislature resolved that "any expectation that any settlement of the debt, upon any other basis, will ever be made or tolerated by the people of Virginia, is absolutely illusory and hopeless," and that the interests of both creditors and the state required its complete acceptance by both. Not a vote was recorded against this resolution. The Readjuster Democrat Newberry introduced it in the Senate, the Funder Democrat William A. Anderson in the House. Among those who voted for it were A. Koiner and W. C. Wickham, ex-chairmen of the Funder wings of the Conservative and Republican parties respectively.[12] Governor Cameron signed it. Moreover, laws suggested by the governor and designed

There was undoubtedly a great deal of fraud. In most places Mahone controlled the election of judges; and his state board of canvassers refused to go behind the returns. Half the "Southwest," two-thirds of the Valley, and all the cities but Norfolk and Petersburg went Democratic.

[12] *Acts,* 1883-1884, p. 7; House and Senate *Journals.*

to make the Riddleberger Act and the "Coupon Killers" more effective were enacted without difficulty.[13] Nor did the legislature undo or attempt to undo any of the other economic and social legislation of the Readjusters, the more liberal suffrage, the larger appropriations for schools and charities, the lower and fairer taxes, and the abolition of the whipping-post. On the contrary, it desired to supplement and extend them all.[14] For such legislation was, unquestionably, the "will of the people."

If in these matters the legislature followed the Readjuster creed, still more did it acknowledge the influence of the Mahone system in its political activities. Acting upon the pointed advice of the new state committee,[15] individual members forbore to seek offices for themselves, and the caucus smoothly and equitably apportioned the patronage.[16] Next, by prompt and vigorous efforts, the Democratic majority in each house was increased to two-thirds.[17] Then the task of breaking the grip of the machine was begun. The governor's share in the appointment of the commissioner of agriculture and of the capitol police was taken away.[18] The boards of all the asylums were declared vacant and the appointment of their members was transferred from the

[13] Governor, *Message*, December, 1883; *Acts*, 1883-1884, pp. 504, 527; *Acts*, 1884 (extra session), p. 163.

[14] Above, ch. 12. *Cf.* the white female normal school in the "Southside" and the lunatic asylum in the "Southwest," *Acts*, 1883-1884, pp. 417, 692. The House directed that a bill for separate negro teachers and trustees for negro schools be reported, but nothing resulted, House *Jour.*, p. 86.

[15] *Dispatch*, November 23, 25, 1883.

[16] Especially pleasing was the selection of Col. Frank G. Ruffin as second auditor, the officer in charge of public debt operations and of the literary fund and member of the board of public works.

[17] "*New Virgina*"; Ruffin, *Scrap-Book*, II, p. 224.

[18] House *Jour.*, 1883-1884, pp. 274, 752, 754.

governor to the board of public works.[19]   Over the heads
of the county superintendents of schools was held a
threat of fine and loss of office for active participation
in politics.[20]   The appointment of school trustees was
taken from the boards, composed each of county judge,
superintendent, and commonwealth's attorney, and given
to new boards elected by the legislature.[21]   Registrars,
judges, and clerks of elections were treated in a similar
fashion, without any adequate provision being made for
representation of both parties.[22]   The charters of towns
were changed so as to require new registration of voters
and otherwise to aid Democratic control.[23]   The state
was redistricted for Congress, not indeed with such
disregard of numerical equality as Mahone had shown,
but with such obvious political bias that the governor
declared the new arrangement would give one party
seven or eight of the ten representatives on the basis
of the nearly balanced vote at the last Congressional
election.[24]   To justify such strenuous and high-handed
procedure, and to obtain material for the next campaign,
as well as to bring the guilty to bar, partisan investigations were made into every cranny of Mahoneite
official activity.   These investigations brought to light
a mass of incompetence, petty graft, and violent partisanship, and some gross mismanagement.   Yet on the
whole it may be said that the tone of the reports was
rather judicial than partisan and though the terror of
prosecution was held over some, the object in the end
seemed to be to prevent and reclaim rather than to
punish.   Upon the public records, the legislature spread

[19] *Acts*, 1883-1884, p. 155; House *Jour.*, pp. 482-513.
[20] *Acts*, 1883-1884, pp. 684, 698.
[21] *Ibid.*, p. 177; 1884 (special session), p. 119.
[22] Sen. *Jour.*, 1884, p. 23; Acts of August 25, November 29, 1884.
[23] Norfolk, Portsmouth, Danville, Petersburg.
[24] House *Jour.*, 1883-1884, p. 556.

a demand that Mahone, as the instigator of strife between the races, a traitor to the party that had elected him, and a traducer of the state he represented, should resign his seat in the United States Senate. And it sat at this work, at intervals, till past the November elections of 1884, with no little inconvenience to its members and at the risk of a popular reaction.[25]

Meantime Mahone fought what was perhaps his most brilliant campaign. In point of intelligence and respectability the "Coalitionist" state convention of April 23, 1885, was undoubtedly the strongest that he had ever got together. A flag of the United States draped the chairman's platform, and around the arch behind, one could read, "With malice to none, with charity to all." Matters moved with clock-like precision. Governor Cameron's administration was endorsed "like a flash," even though the governor himself pleaded indisposition to the demand for a "speech." Tremendous cheers greeted "Mahone, the black man's friend." "With all the dramatic effect he could bring to bear," Mahone read the platform. In it for the first time the name Republican was officially taken—"the Republican party of Virginia." No mention was made of Readjustment; the emphasis was laid upon liberalism, in state as well as nation. Despite the spirited objection of some who preferred Blaine, the delegates to the national convention were instructed to vote as a unit for Arthur: "We are for Arthur because Arthur is for us" ran the convention slogan which the delegation carried to Chicago. In the only important contest which came before the national convention, the Mahone delegates won over the "Straight-out." And when Wise and Riddleberger, so rumor had it, hoped to weaken Mahone by a rather precipitate "break" to Blaine, the successful candidate

[25] *Dispatch,* March 8, July 29; *State,* March 5, 6, November 29, 1884.

sent word that "Arthur could not have been a better friend to General Mahone than he would be." None the less, at the elections, the Cleveland ticket won by 6,000 in 284,000 votes counted. Republicans cried fraud, corruption, intimidation, and claimed the state by 15,000. Fraud there undoubtedly was, but by Republicans as well as by Democrats. That eighty-five per cent of the total possible vote was counted seems to disprove the charge of extensive intimidation. Acceptance of Readjuster views by the Democrats, the race line, and the probability of national Democratic success, together with the smoother workings of the new machinery, would seem to account sufficiently for the great increase in the Democratic vote.

With discriminating firmness the Cleveland administration at once proceeded to remove or suppress all Republican postmasters and revenue officials who had been unduly active in state politics—one of the things for which Cleveland had been elected, the *Nation* declared. By the middle of July, 1885, the task was fairly complete in the opinion of even so interested an observer as Chairman Barbour. There remained, accordingly, only the governorship to be "redeemed." For this position the Democrats pitted Fitzhugh Lee against John S. Wise, who still maintained a semi-independent allegiance to Mahone. So worn out were the old issues that both parties sought new ones, and these were usually ultra-democratic. Thus both endorsed "local option" in the matter of liquor licenses, both advocated increased pensions for Confederate soldiers and free text-books for the public schools, and both promised a variety of things calculated to win the labor vote. National interest was again aroused: because, said the New York *Tribune*, Virginia was the only Southern state where even a semblance of fair elections was maintained; because, said the *Nation*, ''the whole nation is humiliated when any state is debased by the domination of such a boss.'' For the first time, Republicans of national prominence came down to speak, notably, Sherman and Foraker. Wise polled only 2,000 fewer votes than Blaine had received the year before. But Barbour and Lee raised the Democratic vote 6,000 above that cast for Cleveland. The legislature, too, was overwhelmingly Democratic. So was its successor. And so Daniel and Barbour soon superseded Mahone and Riddleberger in the Senate.

A new and happier era had now clearly arrived. Economic conditions were much better than in 1879. Realty assessments showed an increase of thirty-six millions—more than fifteen per cent, and the tax burden of the farmer was proportionately fairer than of old.[26] There were no railroads now in the hands of receivers. Charters for new and *bona fide* enterprises were being issued in large numbers. The lower middle class continued to increase in numbers and in wealth; over ninety-six per cent of the 300,000 tithables paid less than twenty-five dollars each in taxes. Newspapers had increased in size, number, and circulation; they no longer abounded in huge lists of delinquent taxpayers or in cries from the distressed. Schools were firmly established. In 1886, the literary fund was converted into more than a million of Riddlebergers. A normal school for the whites and another for the colored, the former presided over by Dr. Ruffner during its first years, were receiving regular, if inadequate, assistance. By an act of 1884, appropriations for disabled Confederate soldiers had been increased one-half. There was a disposition to continue

---

[26] Realty now contributed thirty-six per cent of the total revenue, as against fifty-nine per cent in 1871.

work on the asylum problem until no insane person should be confined with criminals.

Old sectional antipathies among the upper classes had been greatly modified. Scalawags and carpet-baggers were almost entirely things of the past; their Mahoneite successors were at last muzzled. For the first time in almost a generation, "real Virginians" now had a share in the national government. They helped in the making of the laws, and they alone executed the laws within the state. They had the ear of the president. They even represented the nation abroad. With manifest pleasure, they saw the independent political opinion of the North approving their political position, and they rejoiced that the commercial world at last understood and applauded the "Bourbon" stand for the fiscal honor of the state. They found parental pride in the applause with which Fitzhugh Lee was welcomed during the presidential inaugural parade, and their press chronicled without unfavorable comment the fact that in the following July he spoke at Bunker Hill. Warmed now by the generous attitude of Grant at Appomattox and again in 1869, a Democratic convention paused, on news of his death, to adopt resolutions of respect and sympathy. "Surely," said the *Dispatch,* "we have a united country." "Best of all," said the *Whig,* in summing up Colonel Elam's interpretation of the Readjuster Movement, "it gave us that political regeneration which makes us New Virginians indeed, by transforming us from mere Virginians and Southerners into American citizens."

But the fiscal situation was still serious. All except one of the state's former holdings in internal improvement companies were gone. The revenues, even after the reassessment of realty in 1885, showed but little increase over those of 1875. They could scarcely be

increased. For even if a statesmanlike policy would
permit the imposition of a greater burden upon the
masses, political conditions would not: Mahone, men
said, had ''corrupted the people.'' Nor could the tendency to reach out and tax capital be pursued far; for
capital had not entirely forgiven the repudiating state,
and, besides, the Democratic party must draw upon capital in order to maintain its control. On the other hand,
there were new and increased expenses. Some of these
were temporary: the extra legislative expenses, for example, and possibly the increased criminal expenses. But
others were unquestionably permanent: such as those
for schools, asylums, and pensions. In general, it was
quite clear that any increase, present or prospective,
in the revenues of the state, as compared with the period
of 1877-1879, was fully offset by present and prospective
expenses that, for all practical purposes, could not be
avoided. Obviously, the debt was still an important consideration. Even under a complete funding into ''Riddlebergers'' the interest would be hard to meet. So far,
however, less than five millions had been funded, and
creditors showed no inclination to increase the amount.
But public sentiment on this question was almost unanimous now. When part of the legislation supplement-
ing the ''Coupon-Killers'' was declared unconstitutional,
other was contrived. Business men refused to use the
old coupons, lawyers to take coupon cases. The bondholders did, indeed, make a strong and spectacular legal
fight, during which attorneys for both sides were in
turn sent to prison for contempt.[27]   But by degrees it
became clear that the state was slowly winning: between
1883 and 1890 the maximum amount of coupons received
at the treasury for one year was $258,938, the minimum,

[27] For an account by the most energetic and daring of the bondholders'
counsel, see Royall, *Some Reminiscences.*

$40,540. So the holders of consols and ten-forties yielded. By agreeing to the act of February 20, 1892, they accepted the essential principles of the Riddleberger Act.[28] The new bonds were known as "centuries"; the act, as "the settlement." There remained the task of compelling West Virginia to settle with creditors for her share of the old debt; this was a moral obligation assumed as part of "the settlement." But the economic and fiscal problem of Virginia was at last solved.

Though Mahone's control over the state was never restored, the Republican party retained its newly won supremacy in over one-half of the "Southwest" and about one-third of the Valley and in the cities of Norfolk and Petersburg. It was more strongly entrenched than of old in the rest of the "Southwest" and the Valley. In the "East" it once more controlled in most of the counties with large negro majorities and in some cases where the negroes were not in the majority. Improvement in Republican leadership was noteworthy throughout the state. But the quality of its masses improved little in the "East." Over this party Mahone's personal domination continued, though his most trusted lieutenants left him. Defeat did not crush his spirit or destroy his unique prestige in national politics.

The Democratic party in Virginia did not recede from

28 See Governor, *Message*, January 14, 1892, and accompanying documents. The commission representing Virginia consisted of P. W. McKinney, R. H. Cardwell, H. T. Wickham, J. Hoge Tyler, Taylor Berry, W. D. Dabney, and Robert H. Tyler. F. P. Olcott was chairman of the bondholders' committee. Grover Cleveland, Thomas F. Bayard, E. J. Phelps, George S. Coe, and George G. Williams constituted an "advisory board for the creditors." Some points which the Readjusters had insisted upon were not incorporated in the settlement, e.g., subjection of the new bonds to taxation.

its newly assumed preference for popular wants as against the interests of the creditors. Nor for fifteen years did it dare again legally to restrict the suffrage though disgust with the negro voter became more and more profound. The new plan of organization and the new methods of conducting campaigns were not abandoned. The new leaders were not discarded. If in time control became unduly concentrated and dangerously close to large business interests, it was never again distinctly Bourbon or neglectful of the new man and the young man. When the national Populistic movement came, the way had already been prepared for its acceptance by the Democrats. In short, the Democratic party, as compared with the old Conservative party, its predecessor, was new in organization, methods, ideals, and leadership. These changes, constituting a compromise between "Radicalism" and the "Old Régime," would probably have come without the "Readjuster Movement." But to tell how they did occur has been the purpose of this study.

CONCLUSION

Post-bellum Virginia history may be said to end with
1885: the ten or twenty years succeeding constitute an
appendix, which may be included or omitted without
material difference.

The task of the period (and its test) was internal
readjustment—readjustment of the state's economic and
social policies, of private enterprises and ideals, and of
the relations of races, classes, and sections.

Most of these problems were solved with but little
friction owing to the domination of Conservatism. For
Conservatism was not only a political party, it was also
a social code and a state of mind which bound the whites
to united and temperate action. The solution was accomplished, however, under a condition of stress—of potential conflict between aristocratic and democratic forces.
The aristocratic forces comprised partisans of the old
régime, weakened by emancipation, indeed, but strengthened by firm alliance with capitalistic interests and by
the gradual development of an "old soldier" cult. The
democratic forces were the "West" and the "new"
men whom war and reconstruction had thrust forward in
the "East." They included also the "poor whites" and
the freedmen; but these groups were usually impotent
because of race antagonism.

The Radicalism of reconstruction days and the Readjuster Movement a decade later were both democratic
protests against the domination of Conservatism. Radicalism, however, was largely obstructive of genuine democratic advance because it was exotic and rested upon
force, and because it alienated the "West" through its

attitude toward the negro. The Readjuster Movement, on the other hand, was native in origin, and its democracy was meant primarily for the whites, the negroes being considered inferior allies. Each succeeded a well-defined aristocratic movement, and each ended in a compromise whereby Conservatism became more democratic and more progressive.

On detailed analysis, the Readjuster Movement exhibits a political, an economic, and a social phase. Not until the breakdown of reconstruction politics, through the continued defeat of the Republican party and the overgrowth of the Conservative, could independent opinion make headway. Then the union of Conservative "outs" with the Republican fragments as "Readjusters" was feasible. This, in turn, paved the way for an enlarged and rejuvenated Republican party and, indirectly, for a Democratic party that was smaller but better organized and more liberally led than its Conservative predecessor.

It was economic depression that led most directly through the consequent fiscal embarrassment and general discontent, to the reception of the inciting principle of the movement. This principle, that the state's creditors should be compelled to share in the general loss occasioned by war and reconstruction, gave the movement its name. Other things being equal, it was supported by the hardest-pressed individuals and communities. Eventually it became, through general acquiescence, the basis of debt settlement. Organized just as the lowest point of depression was passed, the movement ended soon after the turn of the tide had become obvious.

Socially, the movement aimed at a government in closer "touch with the people." It sought, specifically, taxation according to ability, unrestricted manhood suffrage, abolition of the special privileges of bondholders, "brokers," and officeholding "rings," and equalization of opportunity through elementary state socialism. The leaders were mainly self-made men of the middle class, marked by energy and political shrewdness. Their methods included agitation, disregard of precedent and judicial decisions, a spoils organization, and, eventually, a boss. The response of the white masses was loud and strong in the democratic "West"; in the "East," doubtful and hesitating. The end of the movement found many "new" men in prominent places. It also found the "will of the people" accepted as the criterion of public policies, and the discovery and organization of that will recognized as the first duty of party leaders. For a short time the negro seemed about to become a part of this political "people"; but the habit of implicit obedience to overseers and a boss proved too strong. These results seemed to necessitate, and to anticipate, the elimination of the negro as a voter and a wider extension of the state's social activities, especially in education.

Lastly, our study affords an illustration of the interplay of local independent movements and national politics. Undoubtedly Greenbackism aided in the inception of Readjustment, and Readjustment prepared the soil for Populism in Virginia. On the other hand, Republican supporters of the national credit and of the great private "interests" aided repudiation in Virginia; and the combination of ignorance in Virginia and federal patronage under a boss made possible the only political breach yet made in the new "Solid South."

BIBLIOGRAPHICAL NOTE

This note indicates the nature of the material used. No attempt is made at a complete enumeration.

MONOGRAPHS

C. H. Ambler, *Sectionalism in Virginia from 1776 to 1861* (1910), H. J. Eckenrode, *Political History of Virginia during the Reconstruction* (1904), and J. P. McConnell, *Negroes and Their Treatment in Virginia, 1865-1867* (1909), furnish the political background subject to the limitations implied in their titles. G. W. Dyer, *Democracy in the South before the Civil War* (1905) is incomplete but suggestive. For the economic and social side the above, B. W. Arnold, *History of the Tobacco Industry in Virginia from 1860 to 1894* (1897), and the contributions of Bruce, Dyer, Clark and others in *The South in the Building of the Nation* (1909) have been used. William A. Scott, *The Repudiation of State Debts* (1893) roughly sketches the debt history to 1893. George W. Green in Lalor's *Cyclopedia of Political Science*, article "Repudiation," and R. P. Porter in the *History of State Debts* (Vol. VII of the tenth census) give useful summaries of debatable figures. Semi-historical in its treatment is F. A. Magruder, *Recent Administration in Virginia* (1912), which appeared too late to be of any considerable service. A. D. Mayo, *Common School Education in the South* (Commissioner of Education, Report, 1901, I, Ch. XI) gives a convenient and suggestive account, largely of the work of Dr. Sears, down to 1876.

AUTOBIOGRAPHIES, MEMOIRS, ETC.

As yet works of this character either end with the war or keep as far as possible from Virginian movements and conditions. There are some exceptions. Wm. L. Royall, *History of the Virginia Debt Controversy* (1897) is the work of a native attorney for the bondholders; his *Some Reminiscences* (1909) presents the mature views of an ardent young participant of the old school. Col. R. E. Withers, Lieutenant-Governor and United States Senator, hated Mahone as much as he could hate anyone, and his delightful *Autobiography of an Octogenarian* (1907) reflects this as well as some slight lapses of memory. Governor Charles T. O'Ferrall came from west of the Blue Ridge and in the early '70's was a Readjuster—perhaps this, perhaps his native kindliness, tempered the tone of his *Forty Years of Active Service* (1904). John Goode, Congressman and president of the last constitutional convention, was in the thick of most of the political fights, but his *Recollections of a Lifetime* (1906) tells little of them. *The Autobiography of John E. Massey* (1909) is valuable for the spirit of Massey and for his writings and speeches, but it is marred by the failure of the editor to indicate which parts of it are of her composition; much of it appears to be compiled from the Richmond *Whig.* Alderman and Gordon, *J. L. M. Curry;* T. C. Johnson, *Robert L. Dabney;* and *Memoirs of Gov. William Smith,* contain important material. Of outsiders who touch Virginia affairs, A. K. McClure (*Recollections of Half a Century* and *The South: Its Industrial, Financial and Political Conditions,* 1886) and Hugh McCulloch (*Men and Measures*) are consistently friendly to the anti-Readjuster, or Funder, element, with whom they were at times associated in business; T. C. Platt (*Autobiography*) saw only Republican machine interests; James G. Blaine (*Twenty Years in Congress*) and John Sherman (*Recollections of Forty Years*) changed sides and views according to party exigencies.

CONTEMPORARY UNOFFICIAL PUBLICATIONS

The State press mirrors, but with much concealment and distortion, every feature of the period. To an unusual degree the Richmond newspapers dominated the rest. Long before the war, began the rivalry of the *Enquirer* and the *Whig,* both dictators of opinion, while the *Dispatch* was an humble gatherer of news. After the war, the news capacity, business sense, and political instinct of the *Dispatch* made it (under the direction of Ellyson and Cowardin) the most prosperous and influential. The *Enquirer* became the organ of the bondholding and aristocratic faction, suspending in 1877. The *State,* founded in 1875 by J. Hampden Chamberlayne and edited by himself and Packard Beirne, succeeded after a fashion to the *Enquirer's* views and clientage. The *Whig* identified itself with the Readjuster movement and the fortunes of General Mahone, and expired in 1888. The Virginia State Library has preserved and listed these; slight gaps may be filled at the Congressional Library, with the apparent exceptions of the *Whig* of 1875 and the *Enquirer* of July-November, 1876. Others preserved and listed in the Virginia State Library are: *The Southern Planter and Farmer* (1872-1876); *The Commonwealth* (Funder, daily, William L. Royal editor, February-July, 1880); *The Religious Herald* (Baptist, weekly, 1870-1882—other numbers in the library of Richmond College); the *Southern Churchman* (Episcopalian, weekly, 1880-1882); the *Educational Journal of Virginia* (organ of the Virginia Educational Association after November, 1869, edited by C. H. Winston, monthly; later the semi-official and then the official organ of the state board of education). Preserved and listed by the Norfolk public library are: *The Norfolk Landmark* (Conservative, liberal, daily, James Barron Hope editor, M. Glennan managing editor) and *The Norfolk Ledger* (Conservative, daily). Typical town papers are *The Virginia Herald* (1871) and *The Virginia Star* (1877-1879), Conservative semi-weekly, Fredericksburg, which were loaned to me by Judge A. T. Embrey of that town. The Northern Neck *News* (1880, weekly, Conservative, edited in part by Wm. A. Jones, preserved in its office at Warsaw) is representative of the country newspapers. No Republican state papers appear to be extant except the *Southern Intelligencer* (1880, Richmond, daily, John R. Popham editor, in the Virginia State Library) and the Valley *Virginian* (1881-1884, Staunton, H. H. Riddleberger editor, weekly, in the Congressional Library). Of outside papers the *Nation* is valuable for the independent (though ill-informed) Northern view. New York dailies followed political situations closely but not with either accuracy or fairness.

Even more partisan was the *National Republican* (Washington), a "Mahone sheet." The magazine literature (which treats the legal side of the debt question chiefly) is unimportant; it is sufficiently indicated in Scott, *Repudiation of State Debts,* pp. 272-274. Few pamphlets of the earlier period remain; many of the later have recently come to the State Library. The views of Readjusters who refused to follow Mahone into the Republican party are presented with great fullness by Frank G. Ruffin[1] and, to a less extent, by A. M. Lybrook,[2] the former previously a Democrat, the latter previously a Republican. Gilbert C. Walker and C. U. Williams present early Funder opinions on the debt. *"New Virginia"* (published originally in the *Whig* in 1885 and probably the work of its editor, W. C. Elam, or of S. B. French) gives a review of the entire period in the light in which Mahone wished the North to see it. This was loaned me by Judge Goolrick, of Fredericksburg. The others are in the Virginia State Library. *American Politics* (1882) by Thomas V. Cooper and Hector T. Fenton, of Pennsylvania, contains an unusually bold statement of the Camerons' share in the events of the later period. Nine editions of this book were issued by 1885 with the account unchanged. For election returns and party affiliations of legislators the *Warrock-Richardson Almanac* is invaluable. The *Proceedings* of the State Grange (State Library, 1874-1876) should be studied in connection with the *Southern Planter.*

OFFICIAL PUBLICATIONS

The usual state publications are practically complete in the State Library. They are often badly digested and partisan. The *Annual Reports of Boards, Officers and Institutions* contain: Reports of the Auditor, the Second Auditor, the Treasurer,

[1] His pamphlets, largely reprints of newspaper articles, are cited as: *Mahoneism Unveiled* (no date, probably 1882); *An Appeal* (1883); *Facts, etc.* (1885, "Facts, Thoughts and Conclusions in regard to the Public Debt of Virginia"). Colonel Ruffin is unusually accurate in his facts and thoroughly honest. His *Scrap-Book* in five volumes is also in the State Library.

[2] Judge Lybrook's pamphlet (cited as *Mahonism Unveiled*) is a reprint of his letter to the *Dispatch* (1882).

the State Superintendent of Public Instruction (also published separately as *Virginia School Reports*) and the various boards of which the Sinking Fund Commission, the Board of Public Works (continued by the Railroad Commissioner from 1877 and published separately), and the trustees of various asylums, colleges, etc., are most important. *House Bills, 1881-1882,* is incomplete but valuable. There is an *Index to the Acts of the Assembly* in their manuscript form (in which they are known as ''Enrolled Bills''). The House and Senate *Journals* contain the governor's messages and other documents, usually as an appendix. Major ''Jed'' Hotchkiss published under authority of the legislature a *Summary of Virginia, Geographical and Political,* which is valuable for its maps. Contested elections for state officers were occasionally presented as House or Senate documents; those for federal offices are easily accessible through C. H. Rowell's *Historical and Legal Digest.* The figures given in the returns of the United States census officials cannot be considered more than approximations, as these officials were often untrustworthy. The *Ku Klux Committee Report* (House *Reports*, 42 Cong., 2d sess., no. 22, pt. 1) is negatively valuable.

MANUSCRIPTS

The large collection of *Ruffner Papers* was placed unreservedly at my disposal by Dr. and Mrs. R. F. Campbell, of Asheville, N. C. For selections from the *Fulkerson Papers* and the *Dickinson Papers,* I am indebted to Mr. S. V. Fulkerson, of Bristol, Virginia, and Miss Camilla Dickinson, of Richmond. J. Willcox Brown, of Afton, Virginia, has recently deposited with the Virginia State Library a collection of manuscript articles, in the nature of recollections, by himself. The *Harvie Papers,* discovered by Prof. C. H. Ambler and deposited in the State Library by Dr. Armistead G. Taylor,[3] contain letters from Gen. William Mahone and other Readjusters to Col. Lewis E. Harvie, of Amelia County and Richmond. The large and carefully preserved collection of *Mahone Papers,* hitherto inacces-

[3] See Report of the Virginia State Library for 1913-1914, p. 7.

sible to students, was, through the courtesy of Mr. and Mrs. W. L. McGill, placed at my disposal for consultation on crucial points. The state *Land Books* are invaluable for an understanding of economic conditions. Under the enlightened and energetic policy of the State Library's present management other similar material will probably soon be available.

"PERSONAL RECOLLECTIONS"

Under this title are entered memoranda of conversations with men who were participants in the situation described but whose names it is not advisable to give at present.

INDEX

INDEX